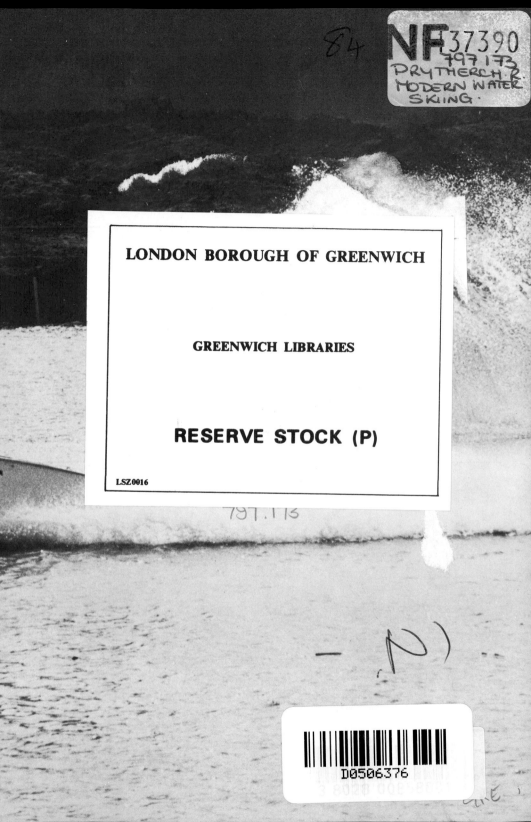

Modern
Water Skiing

Companion volumes

BACKPACKING EQUIPMENT
Making It and Using It
G. R. Birch

ADVENTURE CYCLING
In Britain
Tim Hughes

Modern Water Skiing

A Guide for Skiers and Boat Drivers

Reginald J. Prytherch

BLANDFORD PRESS
Poole   Dorset

First published 1979 by Blandford Press Ltd.

Copyright © 1979 Blandford Press
Link House, West Street
Poole, Dorset BH15 1LL

British Library Cataloguing in Publication Data

Prytherch, Reginald John
   Modern water skiing.—(Adventure sports series).
   1. Water skiing
   I. Title   II. Series
   797.1'73   GV840.S5

ISBN 0 7137 0927 8

Filmset in 11/12 Baskerville and
printed in Great Britain by
BAS Printers Limited, Over Wallop, Hampshire.
Bound by Robert Hartnoll Ltd., Bodmin

Contents

Acknowledgements

While writing this book I spoke with many long term friends in water skiing and would like to record my thanks to them all for the up-to-date information they passed on to me.

Special thanks are due to Jill Hill of the British Water Skiing Federation and to David Nations, the British National Water Ski Coach, who still found time to discuss water skiing with me during the year when he saw his prodigy, Mike Hazelwood, become overall World Water Skiing Champion.

I am most grateful to Margaret and David Kathro who not only supplied and drove the ski boat, but helped with the instructional photographic sessions, and to their children Jennifer and Robert, who kindly demonstrated the actual skiing.

I am indebted to Philip T. Smith who took the majority of the photographs and to Paul Curtis who did the line drawings.

My thanks are also due to Leslie Bryce and Sheila Doeg of *Waterways News* without whose help some of the figure skiing photographs would have been difficult to obtain.

Other photographs are reproduced by courtesy of All Sport/Tony Duffy, Colorsport, Bluebird Marine Ltd, and Donald Healey.

Thanks are also due to Geraldine Christy of Blandford Press.

Finally, I should like to convey my thanks to the staff in my business for their understanding and perhaps when they read this book they will realise why I kept disappearing in 1978.

R.J.P.

Part One

BOATS AND EQUIPMENT

As far as I know none of the World's Water Ski Federations or Associations have carried out a survey to ascertain how people try water skiing for the first time. If one has then I offer my apologies, and I would expect the results of such a survey to show that about fifty per cent tried whilst on vacation and fifty per cent either through clubs or with a friend who owns a boat. The latter group almost certainly would have carried on and become good all-round water skiers whilst many of the former would have had to drop out because of lack of facilities in their own residential area.

When I first considered writing this book I thought of aiming only towards the 'first-timers', whether on two skis or one, but with twenty years of teaching water skiing now behind me I remembered the number of people I had taught and who then carried on as family water skiers. By this I mean the people who buy boats and mostly ski with their family and friends. Often the skier I taught only carried on for a few more times, but then married, had a family and later purchased a boat, thus becoming one more member of the growing world population of 'family water skiers'.

Gradually I realised that many of these boat owners and would-be owners really knew very little about driving the boat for water skiing. As I have witnessed several times over many years around coasts all over the world, it is often a case of the 'blind leading the blind' as the boat owner and his 'family' skier have not the faintest idea on how to go about the sport of water skiing safely. Many other books have of course been written about water skiing, but few even mention the driver; indeed I was

7

guilty of this in a book I wrote some years ago and so in this book I have tried to rectify this obvious error.

The formula I have adopted may seem a little unusual in that I have concentrated on two major teaching parts, (Parts Two and Three), and in these I have tried to explain as fully as I can the sport from both the skier's and the driver's side and then endeavoured to bring them together at the finish of each stage.

I have written Part One more as an introduction to both boats and equipment. It would take a whole book to study the merits or disadvantages of all the different makes of boats and, to a certain extent, water skis available throughout the world. However, I will try to give some guidance on the different types of boats which are suitable for towing water skiers, though at all times the reader must take into consideration the conditions of his or her own area. Let us start by discussing briefly the three main types of power available to the prospective owner of a boat suitable for water skiing.

Inboard boats and engines

Let us first consider the top of the price range and then work down. If you go to a major water ski championship then almost certainly the towing craft will be a boat powered by an engine mounted inboard, amidships. The power units available for this type of craft are usually marinised automobile engines, but over the years almost as much experimental work has gone into their development as the engines found in the average automobile. Indeed, in those developed for use at sea the general standard of parts tends to be much higher than their counterparts used on land.

Whilst the overall cost of purchasing an inboard boat may be considerably higher than that of the other boats I shall describe later, the cost of spares because of mass-production in the auto trade can be a lot less. Also although they are usually more powerful they often have a better fuel consumption, making a further saving after the initial outlay.

The good points

Since in most cases they are larger than the average stern-drive or outboard boat they are heavier and certainly more stable on turns. To be fair the gap between the stability of an inboard as compared to an outboard

8

boat has narrowed considerably over the past twenty years or so, but it is still a factor to bear in mind. This is more noticeable in championships where the boat has to stay on a rigid set course at a certain pre-determined speed while it is pulling a slalom skier or a skier preparing to jump over a ramp. A quick word here, if I may, on behalf of my friends in the water ski world who drive in international competitons. If you *are* lucky enough to see a major competition spare a little time from watching the skier to admiring the handling of the boat by the driver. These few top competition drivers are often forgotten, but they are masters at their craft and it is due to their skill that the world records and fantastic achievements attained by skiers in competitions are of such a high standard as they are today.

We have ascertained, therefore, that inboard boats are more stable. The turning behaviour is usually exceptionally good as they have the addition of a rudder. Turning, as with all power boats at both slow and high speeds, is helped by the use of the power of the engine. When driving a large inboard ski boat at low speed the use of the throttle to assist turning is all-important and takes considerable practice.

The towing bracket on an inboard boat is usually mounted on a pole just behind the driver in the centre of the boat. This enables the rope handler to control the rope without moving around the boat which in turn makes handling of the boat easier. Without a doubt this position for the mounting is the best for all types of water skiing, but it is not a practical position on many family 'runabouts', especially those with outboard motors. The skier gains by having unrestricted swing on the mounting and it is rare for the rope to catch on any part of the boat as it is usually mounted much higher than the stern end of the boat. With outboard boats where the rope is attached to cleats either side of the transom or on a pulley system the rope often snags and pulls the skier off balance.

I suppose to the layman the first problem when considering an inboard boat is the price, but if one swallows hard and perhaps approaches an accommodating bank manager this may be a problem which disappears. The major snag with an inboard boat is

The problems

9

usually its size and weight. Whilst it is transportable, it is certainly not so easy to trail as an average outboard or stern drive craft. Some of the smaller inboards are fairly easy to put on or take off while the trailer is in the water, but unfortunately because of their size the power unit has to be much smaller. This in turn makes the boat only just powerful enough for water skiing and I personally have found in the past that if they are only slightly out of tune they will not pull, say, an average-sized mono skier, from deep water.

As I have mentioned earlier, they are fitted with rudders which are obviously mounted underneath, usually just astern of the propeller. These two important items on the equipment list have an uneasy habit of hitting underwater obstructions or grounding in shallow water. Although with modern technology a method has been devised of renovating propellers that have hit either an underwater obstruction or have become drastically deformed through grinding over sand-banks, it is not only an expensive exercise (not half as much as having to purchase a new one I might add) but it also means the boat is out of action while the repair is being carried out.

In most cases this limits the good inboard boat to being used either on a lake, where it is kept in a boat-house, or in a harbour at sea where it is kept in a marina. Even with the latter the boat is susceptible to tidal problems and hitting sand-banks etc. and is not really suitable for water skiing from the beach. It does have one advantage, however, and that is that, being large and powerful, it is an ideal boat for taking up to six people to an 'away from it all' water skiing area. With such power one or two people can ski behind while the rest stay in the boat. This is only possible otherwise on the monster-sized outboards or the most powerful stern-driven craft.

Outboard powered craft
Whilst the term 'outboard motor boat' is a slight contradiction as the outboard motor is one unit and the boat another, there is such a variety of engines and indeed types of boats that I am considering the two together.

I suppose most families start with this type of outfit by first purchasing a boat and then deciding on the type of outboard power unit they want. This incidentally often turns out to be the wrong choice as many first time buyers go for an engine only just big enough to pull a skier and end up in a similar position to the owner of the under-powered inboard boat where the engine can be only slightly out of tune to ruin a day's skiing. Whatever your friendly neighbourhood boat or engine salesman may tell you it does not always follow that a 33 h.p. outboard motor will give better fuel consumption than a 40 h.p. or even a 65 h.p. one. It may do so at planing speed without a water skier in tow, but having to hold the throttle wide open because the unit is not quite powerful enough will certainly use more fuel. The parts of the engine will also wear out much more quickly so if your boat is large enough to take the larger engine, it could easily be the best bet in the long run. One other minor point may be the exchange price when you wish to purchase a newer model, as most experienced boat owners prefer to purchase an engine with power to spare, whether it be new or second-hand.

One question asked more frequently at boat shows than any other by would-be purchasers of water ski boats is— 'What is the smallest engine I can buy so that I can use it for water skiing?' Since at most boat shows this question is asked of a boat manufacturer and not the engine dealer or manufacturer, the answer can sometimes be a little devious, to say the least. So let me try to be fair, taking into account the most limited of budgets and the keenness of a family to take up water skiing.

Minimum power

Outboard motors start from as low as 2 h.p., but it is not practical to consider any unit under 40 h.p. for use on even the smallest craft capable of towing a water skier. Even at this power you will be very limited in what can be achieved in water skiing. Although it may be possible to tow an average-sized adult on two skis from deep water, the safety factor of being able to do so with only the driver in the boat makes this size of engine barely acceptable. I feel, as do most safety conscious skiers, that the minimum power should enable you to tow a skier from deep water on either one or two skis, but with both a driver and an ob-server in the boat. So taking these factors into consider-ation it is advisable to use an engine of 50 h.p. or more.

The size of the boat of course determines the size of engine at the top end, but as most outboard boats are between 14–16 ft. (4.3–4.9 m) in length you can usually consider an engine between 40 h.p. as the minimum power and 80 h.p. as the maximum. Anything larger calls for very skilful handling and can be considered lethal in the wrong hands. Twenty years ago you would have had to bear in mind the strength of the boat when thinking of the larger outboard engines, but manufacture has improved so much, mainly in fibreglass, that most boats of the size range I have mentioned will easily take the weight of the larger engines.

Inflatable craft

During the past four years or so there has also been a great improvement in the inflatable boat field both in performance and practical use for water skiing. Much of this improvement has come about through the introduction of the inflatable boat with a rigid fibreglass hull which not only gives much faster planing due to the overall lightness of the outfit, but also makes water skiing possible with much lower power than can be used with conventional fibreglass or wooden craft. As a water ski boat this type of craft could easily be a good buy for family skiers without the large cash outlay needed for the other boats mentioned.

Inflatable craft that can be packed down and stowed in the rear of a car have always been popular, but they are inclined to be difficult to hold on course with a water skier in tow. While they are useful for just towing skiers on two skis they can be very difficult to handle when trying to tow a mono skier. I think it should be born in mind that even though perhaps none of the family can actually water ski when you are considering purchasing your first boat, it will not be long before some members of the family will want to progress from two skis to one. This could mean that to get the overall enjoyment out of your water skiing you may find within a very short time you will have an expensive part exchange on your hands if you wish to progress further with your family's water skiing. If you have already purchased, say a 16 ft. (4.9 m) fibreglass boat with a 65 h.p. outboard it would be a fairly simple matter to change that engine for a 80 h.p. one. With an inflatable boat almost certainly you would have to sell the whole outfit and buy again.

Finally I do not want to decry inflatable craft as they are great fun boats for water skiing. There are times when it is the only practical solution, as in the instance of caravan owners who are unable to tow a trailer to their vacation resort. Estate type cars, such as station wagons, can take a very large inflatable boat when folded and tow a caravan at the same time. It is possible to find a boat that will go on the roof-rack to allow towing and in turn will take a decent sized engine for water skiing, but the size alone will obviously govern the safety factor.

The most recent addition to the high-powered range of craft which are capable of towing for all types of water skiing are those that come under the heading of 'stern-drive'. Basically these are craft in which the engine has been especially developed for marine use and although the actual power unit is housed inboard the drive unit is fitted through the stern of the boat (see Fig. 1). **Stern-drive craft**

These boats fall into two main categories; those that are controlled and propelled by a traditional propeller and those termed 'jet boats'. I will deal with the former first. Stern-drive has most of the advantages of an outboard powered craft in that it can be used in shallow water. This is governed by an electric tilt button or a hand mechanism which allows the driver to push or pull a lever that automatically lifts the stern end of the drive shaft when in shallow water (see Fig. 1). The damage to these units, if used correctly, is quite rare and it means that they can be fitted to much larger craft. This in turn gives power and handling capabilities similiar to the 'competition type' inboard craft, but with extra advantages, such as use in shallow water, easier trailing and less chance of under-water damage.

Another advantage more over the outboard rather than the inboard craft, is that as the engine is housed under cover inside the boat it is not so susceptible to salt corrosion. Most of the spares are very similar in design to mass-produced auto spares so prices are inclined to be more reasonable. Whilst not wishing to demean my many marine engineer friends I think that anyone with a basic

13

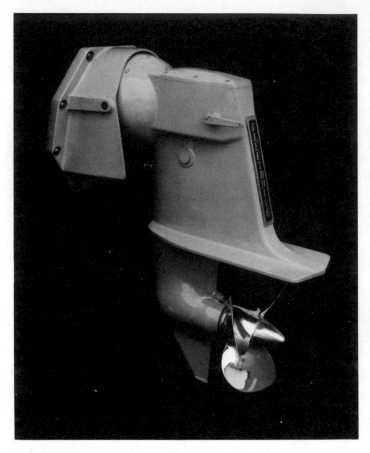

1 Typical stern-drive unit

knowledge of car engines should find little trouble in dealing with minor engine repairs. The outboard motor is a different proposition as the tooling often makes even the easiest repair difficult for the average person without access to a specialised workshop.

The action of the stern-drive engine allows the boat to be controlled with an additional rudder even at low speeds. The drive itself (outside the boat) is really part of the steering as it moves direction when the steering wheel is turned. Although it is fitted with a propeller, the correct use of the engine can make the boat turn exceptionally sharply even in the lower speed range.

There are not many snags in purchasing this type of

boat for water skiing, except perhaps the initial cost. This appears to have crept up over the years until it is now almost the same price as a luxury inboard boat. Some of the most recent stern-drive craft available have all the luxury fittings, in fact, of even some of the most famous traditional inboard builders. The great improvement in this type of engine unit can be seen by the number of international manufacturers who offer either a stern-drive unit or a traditional inboard engine with practically the same craft.

It seems only a few years ago that what has become known as the 'jet boat' first arrived on the boating scene. Jet boats were shown shooting rapids, tearing up beaches and doing almost everything a normal boat driver would avoid at any cost. Maybe it was a way of advertising or at least getting their claims noticed, but in some ways these exploits clouded the issue. They seemed to have numerous engine faults and I think it is fair to say that the earlier models needed such large engines to produce the speed that as a result they were grossly overweight. Without doubt they have now improved beyond recognition and a main feature of this type of power unit is its safety record, especially amongst bathers. Obviously the absence of a propeller must be a big safety factor especially when picking up skiers in deep water. To look at, the unit is similar to a normal stern-drive as it protrudes from the stern of the boat (see Fig. 2), but below the water the system is entirely different.

Jet boats

Both units move with the steering, thus gaining propulsion to port and starboard as well as ahead, but the jet unit needs more power from the engine. Basically the water is thrust in at one end (forward) of the jet unit through an impeller which in turn thrusts it out the rear unit, similar to the way in which air passes through a jet engine on an aircraft. I am not an expert on engines, but it is generally felt that the jet unit needs considerably greater power in order to move at the same speed as a stern drive with conventional propeller propulsion. It then follows that the jet must use more fuel to obtain the same skiing speed, so overall it is not as economical as the other types of power units I have already mentioned. However, taking

2   Jet boat

all the factors into consideration, such as safety to the skier and underwater damage, if you do not mind the extra fuel bills then the jet boat could be the one for you.

**Boats –
summing up**

I feel in the long run that you can only be guided by other water users in your own particular area or at least where you intend to use the boat, but I hope I have in some way helped you with your choice of ski boat. I am sure the initial cost is the major consideration for most would-be boat owners. There are, however, hundreds of owners who would like to improve the power of their boat to enable them to water ski, and there are owners who are thinking of exchanging their present boat so I hope these last few pages have been a help.

If you take into consideration all the major factors relating to power and safety plus the cost of both buying and running the boat without local knowledge you will still run into trouble. When buying a car you must consider whether it will be used for shopping or long distances, and similarly with a boat you should consider where you are going to use it most of the time. If you live inland without the use of lakes or rivers, you will almost certainly purchase for your vacation periods. This means that the trailing and launching of your boat will be as important a factor as its performance, but whatever you choose make sure to allow extra power if you are going to use it for water skiing. Perhaps a minor point, but one which may prove important, is to bear in mind that it is always useful to have somewhere to lock valuables away on the boat.

Finally, I would advise you, if possible, to visit international boat shows and see what is available on the world market, as prices, finish and experience in building vary throughout the world. Collect all the brochures and spend the winter making up your mind and just dream a little—it always helps in the end when purchasing for happy times ahead.

Water skis

Strange as it may seem, although this book is primarily about water skiing there is very little one can write about the actual skis. Over the years there have been obvious improvements, but the overall concept has changed very little. Perhaps the greatest changes, and indeed improvements have been in the more sophisticated mono skis. This is due mainly to competition skiers, but, as in most sports, the knowledge gained through first class competition is passed on in the long run to the general public when they purchase their water skis. Certainly this is true when one compares the hard-wearing qualities of skis manufactured today with those of twenty years ago.

Let us take what is available on the world market and look closest at the type of skis used by the family skier. I shall mention the others but only in passing, as I feel the only type we need to consider at this level are the pairs and the mono ski.

Water skis – pairs

The first water skis that almost certainly you will purchase will be a pair of 'beginner' skis. Over the past few years there has been a move away from the larger beginner's skis to the combination type skis. The original beginner's skis were rounded at the front, but the stern end was usually squared. This gave the skis a much larger planing area than, say, two mono skis. This was essential as very few boats had enough power to pull an adult skier, especially a beginner, out of the water unless helped by these extra large skis. These have been known for years in the water skiing world as 'planks', but this description is a

17

little unfair, as they certainly helped in the days when very few outboard boats were powered with engines over 40 h.p. It is rare these days to see a ski boat under 65 h.p. so the skis in turn have narrowed considerably and from the top look like two mono skis.

All pairs of water skis are manufactured out of wood, with adjustable bindings and two skegs fitted on the underside for stability. These skegs are usually made of wood, but plastic has also been used over the past few years. Make sure when purchasing a pair of skis that the two skegs are the same size if they are going to be used as beginner's skis. Certain so-called combination skis are being supplied with one skeg and a deep mono fin on the other ski. Be warned—these can be dangerous for a beginner as the ski with the skeg will slide over the water on a turn, but the one with the deep mono fin will dig into the water and stop. This is fine if you want to go straight behind the boat and drop off one ski to try mono skiing, but for general use it can be very painful if turning sharply. If the ski with the skeg on is on the inside leg of, say, a right-hand turn, then it will slide on at the point of turn and the ski with the deep fin will dig in and stop that leg moving. This can mean that the inside leg will come up against the outside one and throw you off the skis. If the skis are reversed then the outside leg will slide and the inside one will stay. Such a 'splits' movement can be extremely painful, to say the least.

3   Water skis. *Top*: one of a pair; *bottom*: mono ski

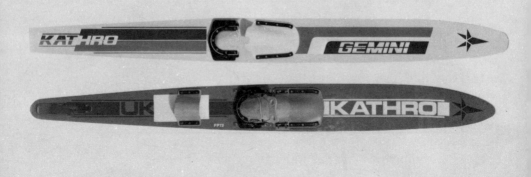

One of a pair of skis suitable for either a beginner behind an under powered boat or an exceptionally heavy person behind reasonable power is shown in Fig. 3. These are the easiest skis to learn on under any power, but in most cases you will want to move on to better designed skis within a very short time. In this case they will, of course, be a poor purchase although they do have one advantage. They are most useful as a drop-off ski when learning to mono ski. So if you have an old pair hidden away in the garage do not use them to mend the fence—they may come in useful one day. This certainly saves losing an expensive ski when learning to mono ski, especially in tidal waters where skis have a habit of disappearing, as you will discover when you have progressed to Part Three of this book.

Combination pairs

Most family water skiers now purchase the combination type pairs for their first pair of skis. These are slightly narrower than beginner's skis; they are fitted also with what is known as a rear bridge. This is for putting the rear foot in when trying mono skiing, normally in a straight line behind the boat. As I have already mentioned, they can be fitted with a deep fin as on a mono ski (see Fig. 3), but it is best if they are used with two wooden or small plastic skegs whilst being used as a pair. If the rest of the family are also up to trying mono skiing there is nothing to stop you from switching to a deep fin and using that ski as a mono ski. I must admit that in fact, however, this rarely appears to work satisfactorily as there always seems to be someone who still needs two skis. The ideal family situation certainly is to have a combination pair, but if you have an old plank ski, for dropping, and a mono for the expert you should enjoy your skiing more.

Mono skis

The range of mono skis is much more complex than that of the pairs as they start with the intermediate skier and go right through for use by the very best slalom skiers in the world. Basically there are three types of mono skis, those with a flat underside, those which have either a concave or tunnel shaped underside and the type usually used at sea which are straked underneath.

Let us deal quickly with the concave or tunnel skis as they are really for experts. Though it would not be correct to say they have no place in the text of this book it must be

4   Mike Suyderhoud in action, World Championships, England 1975

said that to use this type of ski for learning to mono ski presents many problems. They are much more difficult to control on the flat and are in fact designed to be skied on their edges. This enables the good slalom skier to lean over on the turns, just clearing the buoys, as seen in Fig. 4. Skiers of this standard basically ski on one edge of the concave then switch to the other edge on rounding the slalom buoy.

Most beginners purchase a ski with a flat bottom, but, of course, with the deep stabilising fin. Overall this is the most practical type of ski as it should remain steady through the difficult process of deep water take-offs and the first stages when actually up on one ski. There is very little to look for when purchasing your first mono ski as they are all of a similar pattern with a narrow stern end to help in leaning over as you turn on one ski.

The straked or slattered type of ski is mainly used by water skiers who are skiing most of the time in harbours or at sea. They are exceptionally controllable in rough or choppy seas and appear to be more steady on turns when the water is anything but flat calm. They are obviously more difficult to manufacture so you will have to pay a little more for this type of ski, but if your particular area is inclined to rough up from time to time, it could be money well spent.

You will find that mono skis come in different lengths and are often graded to take different weights of skiers. Remember, however, that these weights have been deduced for a skier behind a boat with plenty of power. It is no good purchasing a short ski just because you happen to be short if your boat is under-powered. This problem should not be too serious until you decide to purchase an expensive ski and by that time you will almost certainly be skiing behind a powerful boat. The message really is not to purchase too short a ski as it will make take-offs much more difficult and it can over-tax the engine of your boat.

I will briefly discuss trick skiing and jumping in Part Four, but it is my honest opinion that once you are in this class of skiing you move from being taught to being coached, so I will not dwell on the technique nor the many different types of skis available. Trick skiing at championships is fascinating to watch as the modern top class skiers have brought into the sport not only a very high level of skill but also a rhythmic movement almost akin to ballet.

Trick skis and others

The skis used for these were known as 'turnabout' skis, but with modern skills the actual movement of turning about is just a minor part of the routine. These skis have no fins or skegs underneath and are either rounded or squared at both ends. They are usually purchased without a rear bridge, this being added later so that it is angled to assist the individual skier when making turns on one trick ski. The size is governed by international regulations so some skis are short and wide while others are longer and narrower, since the restrictions apply to the overall area. The short and wide ones are easier to control at first, but no trick is easy and, whilst they are great fun, they are not really to be considered until one is a fairly advanced water skier.

Jump skis are usually the heavyweights of water skiing as they receive a considerable amount of battering from skimming up ramps. Naturally they are expensive, but as their use is very specialised they are not often seen in general sports or marine stores. It is rare to see them being used outside of club activities as the ramp itself is not only expensive to build, but has to be regularly maintained; most ramps are sprayed automatically with water to help the skier pass over the ramp easily. Such expensive equipment would deteriorate quickly if left exposed to the elements for too long without attention.

A last point on the types of skis available—I am often asked why there are no fibreglass water skis. With the exception of some jump skis, with a fibreglass covering this particular material has been used rarely in water ski manufacture. The reason is simply that with the small planing area of a water ski fibreglass will not float. Attempts have been made to build water skis in fibreglass with the inside filled with foam, similar to surfboard construction, but it only needs a slight leak for them to fill with water and sink. Not only is this expensive, but it can be rather awkward if it happens while skiing! So far there is no record of a pair of fibreglass water skis going down with all hands, but many were lost in the ocean depths before they disappeared from the market!

Tow ropes and accessories

The tow rope for water skiing is a very important part of the equipment and an item on which you should not skimp. It needs to be manufactured from a synthetic man-made fibre, and it should not only be 75 ft. (22.5 m) when purchased, but should be pre-stretched so that it stays that length—until that is, you start cutting pieces off with your propeller as most drivers do in their early days of water skiing!

The handle may be either an expensive metal one covered with neoprene and filled with cork, or a piece of wood similar to a broom handle. The former is much more comfortable to hold and is always used in competition skiing. This is the best type to purchase, but must be used with exceptional care as they will soon split if dragged for any distance behind a boat at speed. Most people who ski for fun do, in fact, buy the original type of wooden handle as it stands up to both the dragging and the immense strain of towing a heavyweight skier through deep water.

Plastic handles are available, but although they may be hard-wearing and comfortable they are unfortunately susceptible to snapping at the wrong moment. To be fair to the manufacturers, this is often caused by the 'V' from the rope to the hand being too short (see Fig. 24a), which in turn puts exceptional pressure on each end of the handle, causing it to break. In fact the 'V' between the rope and the handle is very important and should always be at least 5 ft. (1.5 m) from the handle to the point of the 'V'. You will see in Part Three how important this is when attempting deep water starts on one ski.

The other accessories needed for water skiing mostly depend on the type of boat being used. Outboard motors need some sort of pulley system to take the rope centrally from the stern of the boat. The normal fitting is a bar attached to each side of the transom with the tow rope either joined to the centre or attached to a pulley that moves along the bar.

Inboard or stern-driven craft, including jet boats, are often fitted with a central towing point. This may be a pole in the centre of the boat or a very strong fixing point on the top or back of the transom.

Just one minor point regarding the towing equipment—it is helpful both for seeing the rope and feeling for certain points along it in deep water take-offs to fix small floats to the line. These appear to be rather difficult to obtain at the moment, but perhaps some manufacturer will read this book so that once again these ideal safety items will be easily available.

Lifejackets and buoyancy aids

I am not going to dwell on this subject too much as the regulations governing lifejackets and buoyancy aids vary so much throughout the world. It is certainly important to have one or the other in the boat; usually they are the type of jacket approved by a government body, coastguards, Standard departments or a Life Saving organisation, but very few are practical for water skiing.

In recent years the most common type of buoyancy aid used for water skiing has been the waistcoat type. Made from different types of moulded plastic material, these have the advantage of protecting the body in a fall as well as keeping the skier afloat. However, they are often not 'approved' as a buoyancy aid and some may be impossible to purchase in certain countries. Water skier's belts are also made from similar materials; these are very practical and assist skiers in deep water without being too buoyant and making the skis uncontrollable.

There are a few sailing buoyancy aids which may be used for water skiing and which also come up to the required standard for boat safety equipment. However, they are inclined to get easily damaged being dragged through the water on take-offs, but they have to be used in many countries because the regulations demand them.

Wet suits

The use of wet suits in countries with colder climates has been the main reason for the fantastic improvement in water skiing standards (Mike Hazelwood of Great Britain being the overall world champion in 1977). This is true not only in water skiing, but also in sailing, surfing and most other watersports.

Wet suits were designed mainly for use by naval divers during World War II, but it was not until the late fifties that the synthetic rubber material, with which they were made was backed with nylon lining. This in turn made the suits not only more durable, but much simpler to put on and take off. They are now used throughout the world and are as much a part of a watersportsman's equipment as a pair of bathing trunks.

During very cold periods water skiers use a full suit so that they can get full enjoyment from their chosen sport the whole year round. Obviously being fully suited makes manoeuvrability a slight problem, but the modern wet suit has improved so much that this is not so great as it used to be. For the family water skier the two piece suit of jacket and separate trousers is the most practical as the whole suit can be used in winter; the jacket on its own can be worn in spring and you can usually do without it in summer.

As these suits do in fact give protection should you fall when water skiing many top skiers wear a shortie type even in hot weather. These usually have short sleeves with short legs which makes them very flexible so that one is hardly aware of the difference between wearing one and being completely free of a wet suit. Even in the hottest of summers the water can be cold and if you should have to

24

stay in deep water for long they do offer protection against the cold. It is surpising how quickly you can get cold while waiting for the towing craft since it may have to travel a fair distance, pull in the rope and come back slowly for safety reasons before picking you up again.

I would not say that wet suits are an essential part of a water skier's equipment, but certainly more skiers in warm climates are finding their use very acceptable during winter. I suppose to get maximum use and enjoyment from the sport of water skiing in colder climates they are a must, but it cannot be denied that on a fine day there is

5   Ready for cold climate in full two piece wet suit

nothing quite like the freedom of water skiing in just a bathing costume. The time I like best is in the evening when the holidaymakers are back in their hotels, the wind has dropped and the sea is flat calm. The sound of my mono ski whistling over the calm surface and stillness all around are amongst my most pleasant memories.

Part Two
TWO SKIS

While it may seem quite normal nowadays to describe water skiing on two skis as a fairly simple operation, it must be remembered that very few people have not at some time or other seen the sport performed. Most would have seen water skiing at a vacation resort or at least on film or television. I wrote my first book on water skiing in the early sixties, but my first efforts at water skiing were long before that when there were no text books or instructional articles available to grasp even the basic principles. It is laughable to almost everyone now, but we did not even realize that to start one had to be in the water with the skis on. We really did stand on the beach and hoped our very powerful, but exceptionally heavy, inboard speedboat would somehow pull us straight from the beach and onto the surface of the water. I was not one of the initiators of the sport, however. Skiing on water had been achieved successfully years before in the U.S.A., but I first started when I was living on the banks of the Suez Canal. A local Greek businessman had a speedboat that we decided to try to use for water skiing. We made up two planks of wood with bindings, non adjustable ones of course; even the ends of the planks did not turn up at the correct angle as the hot sun flattened them. Still we tried without very much success, as you can imagine, until an officer from a passing ship happened to see us one day and described how he had seen it done in Florida. So we then had a go by starting in the water, with our primitive equipment and rope that reacted more like an elastic band than a ski rope and by the time I was posted back to England we had successfully made the odd hazardous trip across the lake adjoining the canal!

Those were what can be described as early days, but I feel we can now at least assume that all who read this book will have some knowledge of the basics so I feel my role in this part of the book is to help you achieve a sound water skiing knowledge a little quicker than I did many years ago in Egypt.

Starting on two skis

Earlier on I covered the different types of equipment needed so I must take it that you are now ready to try a start on two skis for the first time. There are several ways to launch yourself upon the surface of the water; some are easier and much more reliable than others, but as with most sports it is a matter of progression so I will list them and describe them in order of generally accepted easiness. The different methods of starting then are:
1. The shallow and deep water starts.
2. The dock or pier start.
3. Starting from another floating object such as a rubber boat or raft (I have added this as many water skiers find when on vacation that they need to start not only away from crowded beaches, but from some sort of floating base. This method has its own problems which need to be borne in mind).

Starting on two skis is of course a matter of practice, but there are many 'tricks of the trade' which make everything so much easier than starting each stage completely from scratch. Before moving on let us quickly check our equipment to make sure that we have the best chance of success. May I just say at this point that should you not make a successful take-off first time do not worry. Whatever may be said by compatriots over a cold beer in a bar, not many people do make it the first time. Even those who do usually get into all sorts of problems for the next ten efforts.

Let me consider both the boat and the driver, if he will forgive me, as equipment. The boat needs to be powerful enough to pull the skier on two skis without much effort. You will find later in mono skiing that you will need much more power especially for deep water starts. However, to pull an adult skier of average weight on two skis from deep water takes quite some power, though often not anywhere near the full power of which your boat is capable. Besides

28

the driver it is advisable, for safety reasons, to have an observer in the boat who will act as rope handler. While I agree with all the safety councils that this is a golden rule it is sometimes just not possible to do so. All I can really emphasise is that if either your boat is not powerful enough to take that second person or for some reason you are short of personnel then you must drive with extra care. I am not sure that it is a good idea to ask just anyone along to make up the number as the driver can find that he has more problems with an inexperienced rope handler than with either the boat or the water skier.

The rope and skis need to be standard as described earlier. There are the usual pitfalls such as cheap ropes which stretch when under tension. Skis should be of the correct size in relation to the skier; it is no good having a full size pair of adult skis on a very small child for instance. Firstly it is almost certain that their feet will not fit the binding correctly and secondly you will find that when they are trying to get into position for a deep water take-off the skis will float to the surface, making their control very difficult. Under-sized skis or very pointed models are also more difficult to use, especially if your boat is on the border line as far as power is concerned.

You will find throughout this book that I will try to separate the roles of driver and skier and bring them together after the completion of each operation. So we will start with the skier on a shallow water start on two skis.

Shallow water starts

Let us presume that you are starting from the shore although this method of starting can be used anywhere when you have deep enough water and no other object to assist you such as a pier or dock. Walk into the water with your skis until you feel you are just deep enough to bend down and slip your feet into the bindings without having to do an imitation of a duck looking for a fish. It is best to adjust them on the beach before entering the water, but do not shuffle over sand or shingle; protect the underneath of the skis by setting them up on the beach and then carrying them into the water.

Once you feel the skis are on firmly, but not too tightly, then slowly make your way forward to a position about waist deep where you can sit back into the water with your

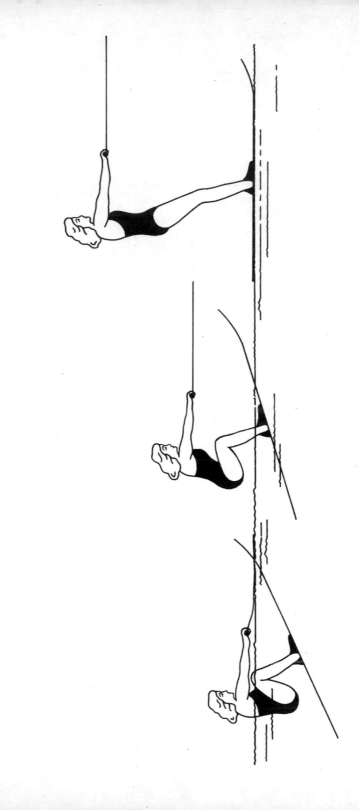

6 Progression from deep water start to skiing position

skis in the 'start' position but with the rear of the skis not actually touching the sand under the water (see Fig. 6). You may find that the moment you sit back into the water the skis will float to the surface in front of you. As long as you have the correct size skis for your weight do not worry, because as soon as you have hold of the taut ski rope a few moments later, you will be able to pull yourself into the correct position. However, before the boat comes near you it is best to confirm both that you are deep enough for this start and that there are no underwater obstructions either just behind or in front of you. This check-out is always essential for the safety of both the skier and the boat driver, especially if you are skiing in an unfamiliar area.

The boat will now circle in front of you and as it slowly turns in front of you the handler will throw the ski rope to you. At this moment you need to be standing on the bottom, if possible, in case the aim of the thrower is not all that accurate. You may have to make a few short, fast steps to one side or the other to reach the rope or if the thrower happens to be something of a marksman you may even have to take avoiding action to dodge the flying handle. It is advisable once you do have the rope, to pull in a few loose coils plus the handle. This gives you some leeway should the driver give too much throttle a little early and catch you before you are in the ready position. You can then let go of the loose coils while keeping hold of the handle and give yourself those few extra vital seconds to get into position.

Providing all is well at your end the driver will start to pull directly ahead of you. As he is moving slowly away start to crouch lower into the water. The aim, which you may find difficult at first, is to allow the skis to float to the surface, with only the points or tips showing just out of the water, at the same time as the driver gets to a position where he has taken up all the slack in the rope. At first you will do this too early and the skis will float either too high or out of position. Do not worry; not only will this take a little practice but, as I have already mentioned, once the rope has become taut then you will have something to lever against to right yourself. You will find that in very deep water where you are unable to touch the bottom a position as in Fig. 12 is helpful; by leaning very slightly

7a   Deep water ready for take-off

7b   Taking up the slack

7c Pulling from start to skiing position

forward with your legs straight your balance will keep
both you and the skis in a manageable position until you
are ready to sit back to allow the skis to float into the take-
off position. Be very careful in deep water, however, as one
of the most common faults with beginners is to fall
forwards into a swimming position which allows the skis to
float up behind the skier. Not only is this most ungainly,
but it is very difficult to retrieve a 'skier-like' position
without one or both skis parting company with your feet.
In water where you are able to touch the bottom, however,
this problem should not occur.

Once the driver is in position, the slack has been taken
up and you are correctly positioned as in Fig. 6 (i.e.
knees bent, arms straight and the tips of the skis just above
the surface directly in front of you and in line with the
boat) you are in charge. Try to get your correct position
quickly, but make sure you feel happy before calling to the
driver to pull away. Remember, especially in tidal waters,
that it is very difficult for both the boat driver and you to
hold one position for very long. You may find under these
conditions that the driver will in fact be pulling slowly

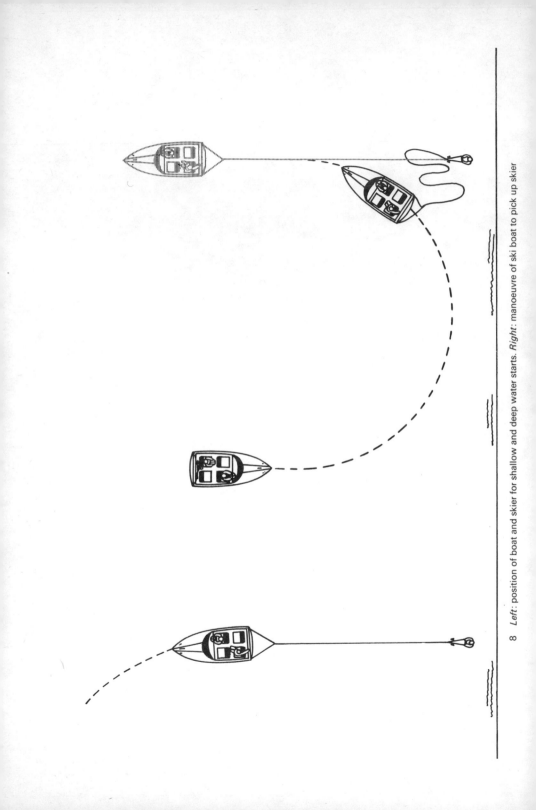

8 *Left*: position of boat and skier for shallow and deep water starts. *Right*: manoeuvre of ski boat to pick up skier

ahead to hold position; this in fact is more of a help to you than a hindrance if you are not in a correct position as it gives you more leverage on the ski rope. The only time it causes real problems is if in deep water you have somehow managed to achieve the 'dying duck' position with the skis floating upside down behind you—then you are best advised to let go of the rope and return to square one! To retrieve your composure from this position with the boat pulling slowly away is a feat reserved for contortionists. It might be worth mentioning at this point that if you have any doubts about your position before take-off such as skis in the wrong position, feet slipping from the bindings etc. then let go of the rope and start again. It is quite difficult to retrieve a decent start position once the full power of the boat is pulling you and can lead to a twisted knee or worse injury.

Let us presume you are happy with your start position and you are ready to call to the driver. The first impression you will get after the driver has opened the throttle will be the pressure of the water against your chest along with the pull on your arms from the rope. If the boat has enough power this will in fact not last for long as you will start to rise on the planing area of the skis and at this point most of the pull is transferred from the pressure of water to the pull on your arms. Also you will start to feel the weight of your body on your legs especially just behind the knees. If you are fit and confident you will hardly notice this, but any weakness here will almost certainly pull you off balance and you will fall to one side or the other. The most difficult position for a 'first-timer' is to know how far to lean either backward or forward. There is a degree of flexibility, but too far in either direction will result in either going head over heels over the front of the skis or between them, most ungracious, or a bumpy ride across the bay on two skis and your rear end if you are lucky. If you lean much too far back once you are in some sort of standing position the skis will shoot forward and you will land flat on your back. The spectators will enjoy a good laugh and so will you when you eventually get your breath back as you are not so liable to hurt yourself falling in this direction than either over the front or sideways.

To help you move from the start position in deep water

right through to the best skiing position in a direct line behind the boat we have tried to show the progression in line drawings (Fig. 6). It is also worth studying the position of the boat from start to finish as shown in Fig. 8 as you must remember that the direction of the boat will be governed by many other factors besides where you want to go. The golden rule once you have achieved some sort of stance behind the boat is to attempt to stay there inside the wake and retain a steady skiing position. There will be plenty of problems coming your way during your first few runs such as wakes from other boats and the turning of your own boat, so it is best to have some idea as to where you are likely to be going, but to concentrate on getting up from the shallow water to a standing position.

Before moving on to the role of the driver to bring him up to the position where you are up in a direct line behind the boat, may I finally say enjoy this part of skiing and savour the moment as you will never again in water skiing feel the same jubilation as the realisation that you are actually skimming across the top of the water on two planks of wood! It is often said that the first time is the best in many situations; certainly in water skiing it is something you will never forget.

Driving for shallow water starts

Whilst the start for a skier is very similar, whether it be in very deep water or from near the shoreline, for the driver it is a very different operation. Let us take the shoreline method first where the skier is able to stand on the bottom while waiting for the towing boat.

The positioning of the boat and the subsequent run in to pick up the skier is almost standard for all types of towing from the shoreline, whether it be for a beginner on two skis or an expert on trick skis. The operation is shown in Fig. 8. As mentioned earlier you are well advised to have with you another person who can act as an observer and rope handler. Briefly his main function is to coil the rope and judge the correct positioning of the boat so that it can be thrown accurately to the waiting skier. He also should watch the skier as he positions himself so that he can relay instructions to the driver on the current position of the skier just prior to take-off. This then allows the driver not only to open the throttle at the right moment, but to keep his eyes well and truly ahead in case of obstructions along the line he intends to take on the ski run. Just in case the rope handler has not performed this operation before let me explain it is fairly simple. He must make sure that the rope is losely coiled so that he can throw it within easy reach of the waiting skier. One essential point which can be ovcrlooked, make sure that the rope is attached to the boat before throwing it to the skier! This may seem obvious, but there are many ski rope attachments on ski boats that have a very simple swing cleat. Once the swing part has been pushed forward by the action of slipping the rope in the cleat it drops back and the rope should pull away from this swing part keeping it attached to the cleat. However, during the excitement of the moment it is easy for the rope to slip partly under this swing bar and on take-off the skier may be left with the entire rope. The importance of the role in which the observer watches the skier as the boat takes up the rope can only come with experience. Often in fact this person is the most experien-ced skier of the trio and is teaching the skier so he is able to pass on precise information to the driver and takes over to such a point that he actually tells the driver when to start thc pull.

The driver is always advised to give himself plenty of room for a start from the shoreline as once he has committed himself to his run-in there is very little chance of correcting any error without having to abort the whole operation and start circling again. This is especially so in tidal waters where the boat has to be under power all the time even to keep in position. If, as in Fig. 8, the driver starts to circle to his port side (anti-clockwise) he needs to circle very slowly until he is sure that the skier is ready to receive the rope. On receiving a signal from the skier that he has the skis on and is standing about waist deep, the driver can pull around in front of the skier at a slight right angle (see Fig. 8). At this stage the rope handler throws the rope to the skier. If the skier catches or retrieves the rope at once the driver can then turn the boat at a much sharper angle so that he comes on to a course that will take him in a direct line in front of the waiting skier. If the skier has to move to reach the rope then the observer must tell the driver so that he can take it much easier and not come

9 Instructor in water holding skier in position

on to the direct line course until he is sure the skier not only has the rope but has full control of his skis. It must be remembered that any quick movement by the skier whilst his skis are on the bottom can easily result in one or both skis coming away from his feet. This often happens with beginners, especially children. The ideal is, of course, for someone else to be in the water with the skier. Not only can that person retrieve the rope, but can also assist in holding the would-be skier in a correct position as in Fig. 9. Where children are concerned this will not only help them get a good starting position, but can also give them confidence. Children, especially the very young can be helped tremendously with an extra person either on the beach, in the water or even skiing with them and I will say more about this later.

Once the skier has the rope and your observer feels he has everything under control the art is to bring the boat on to as straight a course away from the skier's position as possible. As you pull forward you will need very little power, just enough to allow the engine to tick over. In tidal waters you will almost certainly need more as the rule here is always to pull your skier against the tide. If you do not do this then at the slightest problem you will have to take the engine out of gear and the tide will push the boat back over the rope. Propellers have a nasty habit of chewing up ski ropes. This is not only expensive but it can take a considerable amount of skiing time to unravel the rope from the propeller. Modern ski ropes are very difficult to untie and once you have succeeded you will find these ski ropes even more difficult to repair especially while still on the water.

Let us move on and hope you have now slowly pulled directly ahead and the skier is not only in the correct start position, but he has taken the rope handle. You have pulled far enough ahead to take up all the slack so he is holding his balance in the water and is ready to go. Remember now that your observer, although he may be a very experienced skier is not in charge and it is up to the skier, no matter how much a novice, to call for you to start the pull from the water.

The skier's calls

Let me say a few words regarding the call of the skier to the boat driver. It does not really matter what you say, the main thing being to make sure you both know exactly what the other intends. Whether you feel like shouting 'O.K.', 'Hit it', 'Right' or even 'Let's go' is immaterial, but it is best to be consistent and use the same call each time. I suppose as water skiing made most of its earliest progress in the U.S.A. the most common shout is 'Hit it'. I am not too confident about this call, however, as I have known it to get confused with 'Hold it' with either dire or comical consequences. A similar situation exists with signalling to the driver whilst skiing. There are certain signals that are fairly common and in most cases are obvious as shown in Fig. 10 so that once again it is best to have a basic knowledge of these signals in case you are skiing behind a strange boat driver (on vacation for instance), but as long as you and your regular driver are in accord with each other then you should have very few problems.

Once the skier is ready

As you start to pull the skier from the water it is still the role of the observer to give the driver a running

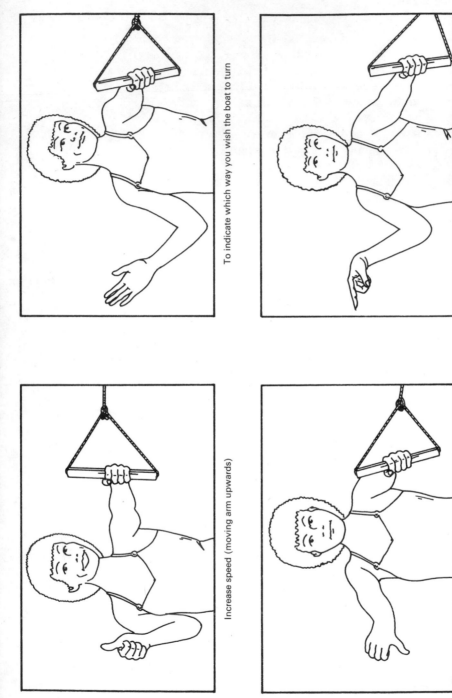

To indicate which way you wish the boat to turn

I wish to go in to land

Increase speed (moving arm upwards)

Reduce speed (moving arm downwards)

10 Signals

40

commentary on what is happening at the skier's end of the rope. It is important to make this pull away from a slow to rapid skiing speed as smoothly as possible so each operation should be gentle. If the skier starts to lose balance he will almost certainly pull on the rope handle. This has the effect of increasing his speed and he will start to overtake the handle. His arms will then be in a bent position, instead of straight as shown in Fig. 11a. To get back into the correct position the skier will release his grip, and his arms will straighten. This is fine, but because of the 75 ft. (22.5 m) length of rope this motion is inclined to be exaggerated by beginners and the result is a pumping action which usually results in the skier falling over the back of the skis. This whole chain of events can be caused by the driver jerking the throttle, although where beginners are involved it is usually a combination of this and lack of balance. The skier is not really relaxed and it is an automatic reaction to pull on the rope if he feels he is losing his balance. A good, experienced driver will feel this and ease down a little to allow the skier to regain the correct skiing position.

Once your observer has given you the 'right away' after receiving the skier's call, it is up to the driver to look straight ahead, but listen for any call from the observer should the skier start to lose control. While the skier is being dragged through the water he will only pull away either to the left or right off course or, if his skis dip in the water at the front, he will let go of the rope. The critical time comes as the skier starts to gain enough speed to move into a standing position. Here any sharp movement of the controls will almost certainly throw a beginner off balance.

Once the skier is in a standing position try to keep your speed fairly even. With a slightly under-powered boat, however, you will find that in using full throttle to pull the skier from the water you will have to ease off gradually once the skier is up, or the speed will be too great and the skier will fall from sheer panic. Always remember to ease back very gently until the skier is planing without any problem and is not holding on for dear life as a result of the speed. Two points worth bearing in mind are: firstly, by easing down on the throttle once you are able you will save

41

11a   Correct skiing position

11b   Wrong position (i.e. showing pumping action)

a considerable amount of fuel, and secondly, if you are not a skier and just the driver try driving your car along a narrow country road at 20 m.p.h. and glance sideways at the passing scenery and see how fast you pass it. That is the speed at which the skier you are towing is travelling on two planks of wood for more than likely the very first time.

So far I have concentrated on starts in water shallow enough to allow the skier to stand on the bottom or at least to be able to walk into the water. Whilst these still come under the heading of 'starts in the water' there are the times when a skier will have to start in really deep water. Usually this is after a fall or if you have to start away from crowded beaches. Once you have mastered starting in any depth of water this can add immense enjoyment to water skiing. You can travel fair distances with one person skiing until tired, then dropping off and another skier taking his place in the water and then carrying on until each member of the boat's crew has had a turn.

Deep water starts

From the skier's point of view there is very little difference in technique from that of starting in shallow water. The position is the same although you may find that it is more difficult to hold correctly until the boat arrives to pull you out. The best method is to stand on the skis as in Fig. 12 with the body slightly over the front of the skis and your arms acting as balancing bars. You can hold this position until the rope is with you and once you have either the rope or the handle it should be an easy matter to drop back into the start position and allow the tips of the skis to float up to just above the surface of the water as in Fig. 7b.

The driver uses an entirely different method of getting the rope to the skier than for either a beach or dock start. With the start in water where the skier cannot touch the bottom the rope is thrown out behind the boat and the driver slowly circles the skier in the water. Once again in tidal waters be careful of the skier, the rope and your boat's propeller. As long as you make a wide slow circle you should have no problem in not only getting the rope to the skier, but he can also use it to steady himself once it is with him.

Driving for deep water starts

12 Balancing on skis in deep water

Skier and driver together

Whilst this is an easy maneouvre for the driver, he must make sure that the rope passes just behind the skier without the boat coming too close. The rope will automatically start to come very close to the back of the skier's head. This is where he must be careful to watch the movement of the rope and make sure that it passes slowly around his head. The skier should take hold of the rope very lightly at first, allowing it to pass slowly through his hands. As the handle end comes nearer to him, (a small buoy fitted to the rope helps to mark this), he should tighten his grip. Then, by using the rope as a lever, change from the upright stance in Fig. 6 to the start position shown in the same diagram. By the time the handle has passed around the back and the rest of the rope through his hands, he should be in the start position.

The boat will continue to pull slowly ahead while the skier adjusts his position and on the call from the skier the driver will accelerate away as in all other starts.

This method of starting is not only the most convenient as one has some chance of staying reasonably dry, which can be quite important in winter, but also once you have mastered the initial pull you are already in a skiing position. The driver's role is very similar to that for a deep water start. His observer should have a simple job in throwing the rope to the waiting skier as almost certainly this type of start will be in water deep enough to allow the boat to come in fairly close to the skier waiting on the dock.

Obviously most docks or piers used are those at lakesides as those at the seaside are either too high for use as a water ski starting point or they are used for other purposes. The dock needs to be just high enough to allow the skier to sit comfortably with the skis resting on the surface of the

Dock or pier starts

13   Ready for dock start

water as in Fig. 13. Slightly lower docks are acceptable, but the lower you go the nearer you are to a deep water start. While it needs to be stable always make sure there are no cross-members under the dock where your skis can catch at the moment of take-off. You will see just how important this is later when you advance to mono skiing with the deeper fin under the ski.

Floating rafts or boats

If you happen to be in an area where it is impossible to use a fixed dock such as at sea you can use either a floating raft or even another boat. The latter is normally too high for an easy take-off but inflatable boats are about the right height and do in fact make good, comfortable starting rafts. They are also useful for leaving the other members of your skiing party who are waiting for their turn to ski.

Both, unfortunately, have the slight drawback that as you sit on the edge you tip the raft or boat and it is easy to slide off before the boat has time to manoeuvre into the correct position for towing. This is not too serious a problem, however, once you have mastered balancing on the edge. If you have friends on the raft or in the boat they can also counter balance the whole operation and make the take-off much smoother. The advantage with using either of these two is, of course, that you can not only get into deep water and thus not have to worry about the boat, but you can often get away from the usual madding crowds.

The dock start
The skier

Once you have settled into the position as shown in Fig. 13 wait for the boat. It will circle just in front, though not too close or your skis may be shortened by the propeller, and the observer will throw you the rope. Once you have the handle section pull in as much of the rope as you can, coiling it loosely as you go, before the boat starts to take up the slack in the rope. You are in complete control once you have the rope, so let out the rope slowly as the boat idles forward. With most ski boats you will need very little slack rope at the time of take-off so you can afford to allow almost all of the rope to be out before you shout to the driver. It is best for a beginner to keep your arms straight at the moment of take-off, although as time goes on you

14　Nearly there. Dock start to skiing position

will start to bend your arms slightly. This not only lessens the impact of the sudden surge forward, but you have less chance of what is called 'dipping'! This happens where, instead of taking off from the dock straight into a skiing position, you dip partly into the water. The correct way comes with practice so try at first to achieve the starting position as shown in Fig. 14 and, if the driver has got up enough power and you get a good steady start, you should move directly from the dock into a skiing position. I must remind you that you will be moving from zero speed to about 15 m.p.h. within a matter of seconds so the pull is fairly hard. You must brace yourself for this, but although it may be a contradiction in terms you must also at the same time try and relax. Do not be too disappointed if you fly over the front of the skis or go off at some incredible angle the first few times as it may look very easy in print, but basically it is harder than a deep water start.

The driver has very little more to learn than for the deep *The driver* water start, though if anything he must be even more careful at the moment of take-off. The move forward after the rope is in the hands of the skier needs to be slow and directly in front of the skier. The moment the skier shouts,

47

the throttle should be opened far enough to pull the skier straight from the dock onto the surface of the water. How much power will of course depend on the engine of your boat, but it will not need the long, sustained pull that you will have experienced when pulling a skier from deep water. You will certainly save fuel and as most docks are situated in lakes there should be no tidal problems. When pulling from either a floating raft or inflatable boat you may find the skier more 'reluctant' to part company with his perch, but do not worry as this little drag will only act as a stabilising influence on the skier's take-off.

Skiing on two skis

As mentioned earlier, once you find you are skimming over the surface of the water then you do know you are at long last really water skiing. It is a great thrill, but as with learning to drive a car confidence may grow a little too quickly in proportion with your limited ability. It only takes a small wave or the wash of another boat just after you think you have the situation in hand for you to find you are skiing one moment and splashing around in the water the next. Take it easy, be content for at least five or six times to be pulled gently by the boat. Stay directly behind, enjoy the feeling and take stock of your skiing position. Try to keep your knees slightly bent to allow them to act as shock absorbers and your arms straight.

Once you are skiing the rope should stay taut at all times, but should you suddenly find you have a little slack do not pull up on the rope; allow your speed to drop and the boat should take up the little slack in the rope. If there is a lot of slack and you feel when it is taken up that you are going to be jerked off your skis then just let go and sink, ready for a deep water start. This can easily happen, especially at sea when the boat hits a big swell and has no option but to slow down. Often the skier can ride over this type of swell better than the boat so if the boat makes it do not worry for you should be able to ride it as long as you use your bent knees as shock absorbers and keep your arms as straight as possible. By straight I do not mean completely rigid as you should be as relaxed as possible.

Outside the wake

Once you feel confident of skiing directly behind the boat (inside the wake) you will want to ski over the wake of the boat to pull along the outside. This is not too difficult, but it must be done with confidence. The faster you cross the hump of the wake the less chance you have of being thrown from the skis. One of the worst predicaments beginners find themselves in when crossing the wake is to wind up with one ski on the inside of the wake and the other on top or outside. The usual cause of this rather strange posture is that the skier has attempted to cross the wake at an angle too close to a straight line. The sharper the angle at which you cross, the more chance you have of crossing over with both skis at the same time (see Fig. 15).

You will find it natural to pull more to one side than the other as with most things in life; it is easier either to the left or right depending on the individual. Take your natural pull and move the skis in that direction by pulling on the rope handle. This will automatically pull you towards the wake of the boat. Remember to pull hard and get the skis moving at a sharp angle to the direction of the boat. Keep pulling until you have passed over the wake of the boat, then slowly pull and turn your body and skis into the same direction as the boat. You are now outside the wake and running in the same direction as the boat, but a little behind and at an angle of 45° (see Fig. 16). The harder you pull and the longer you hold onto your directional pull away from the straight line of the boat, after you have crossed the wake, will determine how far you in fact run before the rope slackens. With practice you will find that you can in fact pull hard enough to overtake the boat, but remember when you do this that the rope will become slack and the resulting jerk when it is taken up again can nosedive you over the front of the skis.

When crossing the wake the sensation is similar to that of riding on a 'Roller-coaster' according to the height of the wake and the position where you cross it. The wake behind all ski-boats is of utmost importance and they vary quite considerably both in height and angle depending on the boat. As a general rule the wake behind a boat with an inboard engine fitted amidships is lower and wider where it reaches the skier's position, i.e.: 75 ft. (22.5 m) behind the boat, than an outboard or stern-drive craft. As I say this is only a general rule as the number of people in the boat and where they are sitting can make all the

15 Skier crossing the wake

16 Pulling to outside of wake

difference. Obviously if you are attempting to ski behind a very powerful cruiser the wake will be huge and whilst this is great fun for the expert it is well left alone by the humble learner.

This should not be a problem once you have made it to the outside, as you simply turn your skis in the opposite direction by pulling on the handle. Again try to cross at a good sharp angle and you should easily ride over the crest of the wake. Usually the wake is inclined to have more rough water on the outside than on the inside, but all this will do is to make the tips of the skis jump a little for a fraction of a second as you enter this rougher water before actually riding over the wake. It is even more important than when crossing to the outside that you achieve a sharp angle as the shorter time your skis are in the turmoil of the outside edge of the boat's wake the better.

When you have re-crossed the wake you have two alternatives once you are back inside the wake. One is to pull on the handle and re-direct your skis to follow the boat and the other is to carry on at that angle and cross the other wake. I suggest you take one step at a time and after one crossing turn back inside the wake and follow the boat before either attempting another crossing in the same direction or crossing the other. If you are skiing in a rather restricted area it is best to make a quick check on the position ahead before starting another wake crossing. If the boat ahead is being forced to make a turn you are advised, as a beginner, to allow the boat to make that turn before attempting another crossing.

As there are no particular points on the actual driving once the skier is up and skiing I will include a few lines on the snags that can occur through bad driving or inexperience on the part of the skier. The driver must keep to a steady skiing speed and try not to make any sharp turns although he will of course be governed by conditions and other craft in the skiing area. However, should he have to make a sudden change of direction he should know where his skier is behind the boat. If he is inside the wake then all that will happen if the boat keeps up a steady speed in turning is that the skier will follow the boat

Re-crossing the wake

Wake crossing – the snags

51

around. However, should he be outside the wake at the time, watch out!

If the boat is being driven in a straight line and the skier is, say, on the left side outside the wake, then a sudden turn to the left will not only leave the poor skier in the helpless position of losing speed because his momentum will have gone as the rope has slackened, but if he is not concentrating at the time and holds onto the rope after having sunk, he will leave the skis and the water in a manner similar to that of the 'man on the flying trapeze'.

Should the driver make or be forced to make a sharp turn in the other direction the resulting spectacle is enough to make the beginner either give up on the spot or die of heart failure. In this case the skier will be hanging onto a taut rope as the boat starts to turn away from the direction in which he is travelling. This will result in a drastic increase in the skier's speed the sharper the boat turns. This pendulum action with the boat as the central pivot and the skier as the pendulum's base needs only to be imagined! While it is a good way of bringing the braggard-type water skier down to earth, it is not recommended for beginners. When I was young and a little more foolish than now, we used to do this on purpose over a measured distance achieving speeds of over 60 m.p.h. So you can see that it can be rather dangerous, especially if the skier is not aware that it is going to happen. Should the skier realize that through no fault of his own the driver has to make a very sharp turn away from the direction the skier is running outside the wake, then hold on until the boat has made its sharp turn before letting go of the rope and gently sinking. It is important, and I cannot stress this enough, never to let go of the rope when the boat is turning at a sharp angle. The sudden release of the rope can not only throw the boat out of control, but may also cause the driver to be thrown out. Turns this sharp, of course, should never be made in water skiing, but one has to bear in mind that emergencies can happen.

Coming in to land

I will deal with this operation in two parts, firstly with the driver's role as his is the most important and secondly that of the skier. It is, of course, a joint manoeuvre and both parties have to be in accord, but the driver needs to position the boat correctly before the skier can manage any control over his landing. It is up to the skier to signal that he wishes to land, but the driver or his observer must in turn signal to the skier that they are lining up for a landing. It may seem obvious that all water skiers must at some time come into land, but believe me, the time may come to end the skiing session without either the boat driver or skier realising it. The skier can be hanging on for grim death while the driver is quite happy tearing around the ocean enjoying the sun and sea breezes.

I remember once opening a water ski school in the early days of water skiing in Europe. The driver was new to the game and he was letting people on the beach have a ski. One particular person who was rather elderly decided to have a go and, to everyone's amazement, he managed to get up from a beach start the very first time and held on throughout a rather long ski. Because I had taken it for granted he would have three flops and go home, I had forgotten to tell him how to finish after his run. It ended with the comical situation of me signalling from the beach to the skier to let go of the handle as the driver ran the boat along parallel with the beach. All I received in return was a sprightly wave from the elderly skier and so the driver had to go around the bay again. Next time the driver was yelling at me to tell the skier to let go and the skier, in response to my yelling and signalling, blissfully waved back and went off on another circuit. In the end the driver had the presence of mind to stop the engine and dump our friend in the water from where he gleefully swam ashore telling everyone how easy it was to water ski!

Landing
The driver

The easiest way to describe coming into land from the point of view of the driver is to say that there is a golden rule which must be followed at all times whether you are towing a beginner or an expert. Make sure your angle of approach to the shore is as near parallel with the shore or landing stage as possible (see Fig. 17). I realize that ski areas near crowded holiday beaches are often very narrow and the angle of approach makes it impossible to stay parallel to the shore over any great distance. However, if the angle is too sharp not only will the skier accelerate as you turn, but also turning a boat in very shallow water is

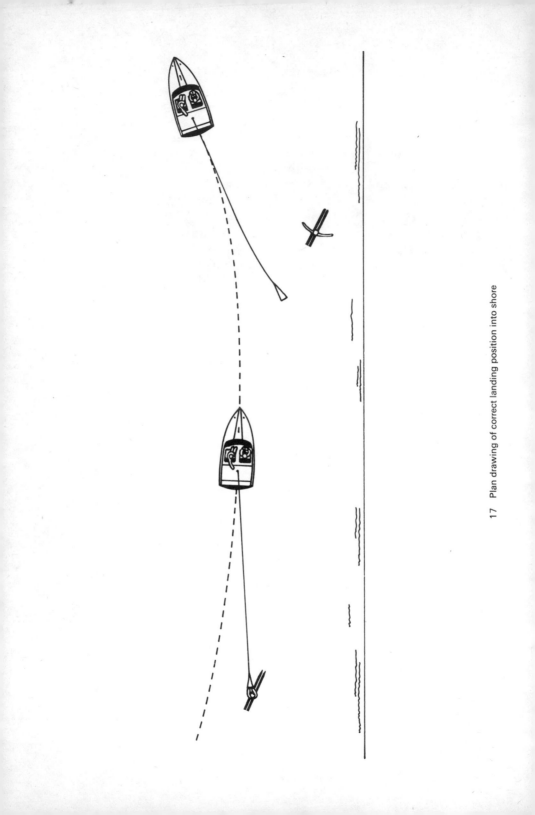

17 Plan drawing of correct landing position into shore

18 Releasing ski rope prior to landing

one of the most dangerous practices in power boating.

If you are able to run along parallel with the shore or bank then a steady approach at normal skiing speed as in Fig. 17 will assure the skier of a correctly angled approach to the shallow water. It is important to keep in mind that the skier is really in control once you have lined up your final approach for drop-off. He will in fact pull to the outside of the wake of the boat and run along parallel to the shore until he lets go of the rope. After the skier has let go of the rope, pull away from the shoreline as in Fig. 17 and start to slow down. This is important as your rope handler will need to pull the rope into the boat. The slower you go the easier is his task, as there is a considerable drag from the rope when travelling at speed. It should also be remembered that the ski rope can easily be damaged bouncing along on the surface of the water at speed. Many tow rope handles are covered in soft neoprene and it takes only a few fast runs with the rope dragging in the water to strip this neoprene from the handle.

Landing the skier is in fact the easiest part in driving for water skiing, but it can also be the most dangerous, especially to other parties in the water. Where the water is shallow there are usually swimmers or other small boats so this is one occasion when the driver must concentrate on his driving and forget all about the skier as it is entirely up to the skier when and where he drops off.

A quick study of Fig. 17 will show you the course of the boat and also where you should be when you decide to drop off. It is a simple matter just to let go of the handle, but it can take a fair amount of practice before you are able to land in both the right depth of water and at the correct angle.

I will take you through the procedure and then add my comments on the various snags and what happens should you not follow the angle of approach as shown in Fig. 17.

1. Once the boat has turned parallel to the shore, move over the wake.
2. Follow the shoreline on a parallel course, watching out for swimmers.
3. Let go of the rope just before you reach where you want to land and you will glide on for a short while, then slowly sink (Fig. 18).

The movement over the wake should be as described earlier, but as you are near land and almost certainly in shallow water you must look about you to make sure the path to your landing spot is clear. Make sure you do not attempt to cross the wake until the boat is running parallel with the shore or you will swing around the outside of the boat and your speed will increase drastically, just when you should be slowing down.

Once you are happy with your run parallel to the shore and you have decided on your dropping off point then turn very slightly in towards the shore and simply let go of the rope. You will then continue to glide on top of the surface for a short while, then as you lose momentum you will start to sink. It is worth noting that on two skis you will glide a lot further than on one, so if you have just seen a mono skier come into a graceful landing without getting wet make sure you let go of the rope much earlier if you wish to land around the same area. It sounds easy, but be warned; there are a number of hidden dangers that can be exceptionally funny to those watching on the beach, but painful to the skier. Let us look at these snags and remember them, it will save much pain and can also save damaging expensive water skis.

First, let us consider the angle of approach and the speed. If you had crossed the wake before the turn of the boat to run parallel to the beach you would be approaching the landing spot at quite a speed. If at the same time you make your approach at too sharp an angle to the shore you are liable not only to shoot into the shallow water at the end of your glide after dropping the rope handle, but you can, if not careful, run right up the beach. When this happens the skis are inclined to stop dead as they hit the bottom. However, you will not—you will carry on at the same speed and, if you are lucky, disappear up the beach like an Olympic sprinter or if it is not your day you will fall and sand-paper your nose rather badly.

The ideal place to land is in shallow water so that you sink to a stop, but land on the bottom with the water level between your knees and your waist. If shallower you risk damage to the sole of the skis, and the wooden skeg or fin under the skis will dig into the sand or mud if you are still moving ahead when the skis touch bottom. For the first few times you are liable to misjudge your angle of approach, but it is better to drop into deeper water and gradually work closer to the ideal spot than go too far in on the first approach.

General advice on landing

If possible it is always best to land where you started from as you should have checked the area for underwater obstructions before commencing skiing. It is important to know the landing area as there are many hidden objects below the surface. One of the most common, of course, is the odd rock, but it is surprising how many skiers manage to get themselves tangled up in all sorts of things. On beaches there are often discarded nets, and the fishermen on the beach will not be all that happy should they catch you instead of an expected sea bass. Lakes and rivers can hide many underwater obstructions and these can be not only a hazard on landing, but can also easily throw you while actually skiing. I have myself been thrown twice by hitting old bicycles and I once landed on an old safe that had been dumped over a bridge. It took a large chunk out of my mono ski!

Tips in teaching children

In Part One I mentioned the use of life-jackets or buoyancy aids. I know that all poor swimmers should wear them, but often they can be more of a hindrance than a help. Children especially seem to have real problems with the extra buoyancy. With deep water starts the aid seems to take over and if the child leans back too far the skis float to the surface and it is very difficult to get them back into position. I am not decrying these aids in any way, but the difficulties experienced with small children make the following tips a big help in getting a youngster on skis.

I am often asked at what age should a child learn to water ski. Of course so much depends on whether the child is confident in water and often this is governed by where you live or the availability of suitable safe water. Usually children who live near the seaside play in shallow water from a very early age and it is not too long before they start to look for other water pursuits. If the child is a good swimmer and not afraid of water, then from five to six years on they are quite capable of water skiing with help from an adult. Most children, however, start at about eight years of age and while they need less assistance there are many ways of getting them started.

Let us first take very young children and see what problems we can expect. Remember they are not only light, but usually they are not too strong. They will almost be able to stand on the skis on the surface of the water. Although this is not practical it means they are up and away in only a fraction of the time needed to pull an adult skier from the water. I have found that it is very difficult to explain everything at once to a very young child so one of the tips that I and other instructors have used over the years is to fix the two skis together at the front. This allows them to concentrate on staying on the surface and not having to worry about keeping the two skis parallel.

If you happen to have a good skier around and your boat is powerful enough to pull two skiers from the water, it is a very good idea to ski for the first few times together. Settle in the water side by side and the experienced skier can hold the rope handle with one hand and use the other to steady the child. This can carry on through the take-off and on to when they are skiing side by side on the surface. I

have used this method often in the past and my way of
gaining the child's confidence is to slip my steadying hand
away once we were skiing. Often the child would carry on
quite happily and not realise that the helping hand had
been removed. Just a point to bear in mind—remember
you will have two skiers of very different weights. This
means that not only will the child rise from the start
position first, and so has to be kept in a crouching position
until the experienced skier is on the same level, but also
this variation in weight can affect the trim of the boat. This
should not be too much of a problem, however, as both
skiers are very close together. It is an entirely different
matter when you are trying to tow two skiers who are some
distance apart as their different weights can easily upset
the trim of the boat. Also an experienced skier and a
beginner rising from the water at different times can make
a considerable difference to the overall handling of the boat,
both on take-off and when turning once the skiers are up.

The best known method of assisting anyone, whether it
be a child or an adult is to stand in the water with them as
they take-off (see Fig. 9). It is surprising how much
assistance can be given, such as collecting the rope and
holding the beginner in the correct position. It looks easy
just to sit in the water with the skis correctly placed in front
with the tips just out of the water. The first few times that
little bit of assistance from someone else in the water makes
all the difference. It saves you falling back and allowing
the skis to float too high in the water. This happens
particularly when the skier is wearing a life-jacket or
buoyancy aid and to lose control is so very difficult to
correct.

If you are assisting a child or adult in the water just hold
their waist and allow them to get in the correct take-off
position, then when they are ready and the boat starts to
pull them, just walk a few paces behind them and help
them keep their balance. With a very light child you can
almost stand them on the water's surface at the moment
the boat takes up the slack in the rope. They may lose
balance after a short distance, but at least they are being
helped through the dragging process where so many skiers
fail purely because they do not have the strength in their
arms.

Finally, in teaching children, it is essential to have a good swimmer in the boat who is willing to go overboard and assist should the child fall in deep water. Tidal waters can be extremely dangerous, even with buoyancy aids on, so the quicker the boat returns the better and if the child needs help and they mostly do for the first few times, then the experienced swimmer should not hesitate in going in to assist. All children find considerable difficulty in getting the skis into a position with only the tips showing when in deep water. This is often because they are using their father's skis which are much too large and continually float to the surface leaving the child struggling to push them down.

May I reiterate and remind you that this 'first-time up' period is the greatest thrill in water skiing. You never again get the same thrill and you will see this reflected in young skiers. They will be very excited should they make a successful run, but at the same time they also are the first to get disappointed should they keep falling. I would not say that every healthy person should with practice be able to water ski on two skis, but over the years I have had very few failures. In all those cases it has been a matter of pure lack of confidence and no amount of teaching will conquer this. Often people fail after a few tries as they have become tired so 'another day, another go' should be the rule.

Part Three
MONO SKIING

Most novice skiers find the transition from two skis to one the most difficult feat they have attempted since they first started water skiing. While there are certain guidelines to follow, which I will describe step by step further on, there are also a few basic rules that must be set down before any attempt should be made at skiing on one ski.

The boat

It may seem a simple point to make, but the number one rule is to make sure the towing craft is powerful enough to pull you easily out of the water. Time and time again I have been approached by family skiers who have failed to get up on one ski behind their own boat. They usually describe it more graphically as being 'dragged halfway across the bay underwater'. Their immediate reaction when I ask whether their boat is powerful enough, is to assure me that it must be as it can tow at least two people at once on two skis. Yet it still will not pull one skier on one ski from deep water.

The drag (weight experienced by the boat) is considerable when the slack of the ski rope is taken up and if the thrust at the propeller is not enough it will not only fail to pull the skier from the water, but the problem will worsen the further boat and skier travel. I often allow myself a smile when I see a boat towing what appears to be a huge wave some distance behind which obviously hides the gasping, partly submerged skier, while in the wheezing, spluttering ski boat the driver is standing up and leaning as far as possible over the bow trying to get the nose of the boat down. Every so often the skier makes a short appearance from his tidal wave as he tries to pull himself from the water.

This is a typical situation with the type of under-powered boat that will almost certainly pull a skier on two skis from deep water without much trouble, but finds the skier on only one ski too much to take. Even with the slightly under-powered boat there are a few tips on attempting deep water starts on one ski, but basically it is easier to try the other methods of skiing on a single ski which I shall describe further on.

Equipment

The other major basic rule again relates to equipment. There are many types of mono skis available throughout the world, each of which has a particular purpose. Often if you are experiencing trouble with your mono skiing it is because the ski you are using is not the right type for your limited skill or for the circumstances in which you are using it.

Combination skis

In many parts of the world a large percentage of would-be mono skiers make their first attempt on one of a pair of skis. This is when one ski is fitted with a rear bridge to allow the rear foot to be placed in a binding. While I do not wish to decry this practical way of making a first attempt, it must be remembered that this ski was designed as one of a pair by the manufacturer. They are known as 'combination pairs', only differing from the usual matched pairs by the inclusion on one ski of the rear bridge which I have mentioned. The stern end of the skis is usually narrower than, say, a beginner's pair as this is a help when attempting to use one of the pair for mono skiing.

Mono skis

A true mono ski will always have a deep fin; the best fins are made out of alloy although some are plastic. The front foot binding is usually slightly further forward than those of a pair. It will of course have a rear bridge and most have some sort of non-slip pad under this part of the binding. Its major asset is, of course, the deep fin. This makes all the difference as it stabilises the ski and stops the swaying movement that most skiers experience when attempting to mono ski on one ski of a combination pair. It is worth noting that most combination pairs are fitted only with a wooden skeg on each ski, as it can be dangerous to use odd fins or skegs.

In Part One when describing the different types of skis available I explained the meaning of concave, tunnel, straked, etc., but I only touched briefly on the main use for each type of ski. At this stage of water skiing as you will be thinking along the lines of purchasing your own mono ski, I will add a little more to my earlier comments.

Firstly you must remember that many of the so-called exclusive skis are intended for the expert skier who usually skis behind a professional type boat with plenty of power. If you feel your towing craft is in this category then you do of course have a much larger range of skis to choose from but I feel it is only fair to warn you that using an advanced model will still make learning to mono ski more difficult than using what is commonly known as the flat or plank type of ski. Once you have mastered the basic skills of mono skiing you will find it easier to improve up to a very good standard by using one of the more sophisticated models.

Flat-bottomed mono skis

Let us first look at the general flat-bottomed ski, similar to your original pair. Overall they are the easier type of ski to learn on as they are as predictable as any mono ski can be. They will hold a steady line no matter what is happening underneath as they are not affected by the wake of the boat or the movement of water. If you ski on a lake or even a river you will not have the same problem as a skier who is learning on the sea. Even so there can still be backwash problems either from the river bank or, on a small lake, the wash from your earlier efforts may affect the stillness of the surface. With a flat ski you have more chance of staying straight in the wake and for a beginner the amount of lean on the turns outside the wake is not so critical as a slalom skier trying to round slalom buoys.

Straked or lapstrake mono skis

Next in order to the plain flat bottomed ski for ease of use is the type that has a build up of wood underneath. Known as straked or lapstrake these skis have a reputation for stability, particularly for sea use. They are exceptionally good when there is a short sea running (where there is only a slight distance between the waves i.e. more of a choppy sea than a rough one). Obviously there is a point where water skiing is not practical on a rough sea, but up to a certain choppiness not only is skiing possible, but can also be great fun. Often you do not encounter a rough or choppy sea when skiing either near the beach or in harbours and the ride only gets bumpy when you get a little way out. In these conditions the straked type of ski is worth using and can be a small improvement over the normal flat type.

Concave and tunnel skis

Most other types of mono skis, including the concave and tunnels, are not only much more difficult to master, but are confined by water conditions to lake skiing. I feel that as it is so difficult to learn on this type of ski we should concentrate on the more stable type of ski. Perhaps when you have improved to the stage where you are able to try actual slalom skiing around a slalom course you will be in a position to consider these more sophisticated skis.

Mono ski starts

Let us now move on to the different methods of getting up on one ski and more important, actually staying up on it. Providing you are now using a boat with the correct amount of power and the right type of mono ski you should now be ready to learn the different ways of transferring from two skis to one. (Just in case you are still having difficulty either with your power source or your ski, I will from time to time put in a few tips that will help you achieve at least a take-off of sorts to get you mono skiing.)

Different methods of take-off

What are the main methods of take off on one ski? There are in fact several, but some are much more difficult than others:

1. The easy way, starting on two skis and dropping one.
2. The deep water start—the most practical way.
3. Starting from a jetty or pier, which needs a powerful boat.
4. The scooter or hop start from shallow water.

All need practice, but I have listed them in order of difficulty so we will start with the method in which we start on two skis and endeavour to drop one.

Dropping one ski

More skis are lost through the drop off method of learning to mono ski than are ever stolen from moored boats. It is surprising how difficult it is to see a single water

64

ski floating on the surface of a flat, calm lake. When the ski is dropped on even a slightly choppy sea it makes sighting the run-away ski very nigh impossible. Sometimes one is lucky and the ski drops off the correct way up and is then easier to spot than if the ski is floating upside down with the bindings below the surface. Skiers have for years tried all types of methods to prevent the ski from floating half submerged. There is the 'weight method' where a predetermined weight is fixed just behind the binding, thus allowing the ski to float with the rear end submerged and the pointed end sticking out of the water. Theoretically this is a good idea, but one has to be very careful with the weighting as with just a little too much the ski will slowly disappear like a stricken submarine. Also be careful if you weight your ski up during your vacation by the sea as you will need to reduce the weight should you want to use it later in fresh water where the degree of buoyancy is completely different. I have seen skis with small buoys fixed to the rear of the ski and I saw one person in the West Indies skiing with a large yellow balloon on the ski. Unfortunately it burst before he dropped it off so that method is not recommended.

What is the best way of getting over this problem? Much of my teaching has been on the coast and not only do you have to worry about the actual siting of the dropped ski, but with a fast running tide you have to have some idea as where to look. We have found that the only practical way is to have an observer standing on the shore or on a jetty whose only occupation is to watch the ski right from drop-off to pick-up. I would not dare to question the honesty of fellow boat users, but it is not unknown for a floating ski to be picked up by someone other than the owner. To be fair, in some cases people genuinely pick up these skis thinking they are lost and it has been known, though not very often I admit, for them to be handed in to the harbour master or some such official. It is some little comfort to find that this, in fact, has been done, especially when your afternoon's skiing has been ruined because you have been looking for the missing ski for hours.

To save some financial embarrassment should you lose a ski, especially if it happens to belong to someone else, it is a good idea to use an old worn out ski. Some handy types make up a 'plank' just for this use. It need not have adjustable bindings, just a fixed toe and heel rubber which is loose enough to allow you to get rid of the ski at the right moment. This type of ski is known in the water skiing world as a Russian ski (i.e. drop-off ski). The plank can not only save you money, but it often also stops the skier worrying too much about losing the dropped-off ski and allows the skier to concentrate on perfecting the technique of switching from two skis to one. It is worth mentioning here that the combination pairs are at a disadvantage, because should you lose one you may have problems in matching up the remaining ski.

The first move in attempting the transition from two skis is to try transferring the weight from both legs onto one while still skiing on two. Stay directly behind the boat and try lifting one of your skis just out of the water. Make sure the tip of the ski is higher than the rear so that it will not dig into the water. It does not matter if the rear of the ski you have lifted is dragging in the water as this will be the way you will want to drop it when you feel steady enough to do so. If you are able to lift it well clear of the water so much the better, as this will give you a feeling of what it is like to ski on one ski. Once you have mastered skiing with one ski raised from the water, then you can drop off that ski.

Almost certainly your impression immediately after dropping the the ski will be that you are far from stable. The ski will start to swerve around and if this action is too violent it will result in you being thrown off. If at this stage you find it difficult to release the drop-off ski the reason could be that either the binding is too tight, since it needs to be much looser than when skiing normally on two, or you are not using a flicking motion to get it clear of your foot. Another point worth noting here is that the wearing of wet suit bootees or socks made of neoprene may keep your feet warm, but they are liable to restrict the dropping of the ski. However, you will find dropping the ski a minor problem and after only a few false starts you should have no difficulty in releasing the ski. In fact after only a few attempts you will not even notice the movement at the time of release.

Remember it will be the deep fin of the mono ski left on you skiing leg that keeps you stable at the moment you drop off the other ski. This is where the combination type of skis are at a disadvantage as they are liable to skid on the surface. It is certainly much harder to recover your balance without the deep fin, especially if you start to slide away from an upright position. Once the other ski has gone there is very little more to do at first other than practice skiing in a straight line on one ski. The only tip one can offer is to make sure you are standing back on the ski and not in the normal upright stance associated with skiing on two skis. An important point to remember is not to be in too great a hurry to put the rear foot in the back binding. First make sure you are on a straight and level course inside the wake behind the boat. When you feel secure just ease your foot into the rear binding. With practice you will find that all these movements will become automatic. The major thing to bear in mind is that balancing on one ski is entirely different to being on two. The ski will not slide when turning as two will, but will dig in so that a leaning movement is needed to turn the ski. I will describe this in more detail later on.

Deep water start on one ski

It is surprising how many skiers give up after several abortive attempts to start in deep water on one ski only. While I must agree this is perhaps the most difficult feat attempted so far, with the right equipment and a few basic rules it should be mastered in a fairly short space of time. Like most starts in water skiing the driver of the boat is almost as important as the skier. The driver should remember that if he gives just a little too much power from the engine at the wrong moment he will ruin all attempts by the skier to get up behind the boat.

Let us briefly check the equipment. The mono ski for a deep water take-off should be either flat-bottomed or straked with a deep fin and, of course, a rear bridge for the back foot. The boat must be powerful enough to pull you out without too much effort and, considering the driver as part of the equipment, the driver must know what the skier is trying to achieve. (Forcing him to read this book if he is not already a competent skier should help!)

The rope   It is very important to make sure you use the correct
type of ski rope when mono skiing, but it is doubly
important when attempting a deep water take-off. Under
the section on equipment in Part One I explained what a
good ski rope should consist of, and it might be worth
back-checking at this point to make sure the rope is a help
and not a hindrance. As a quick check, the 'V' part of the
rope from the handle to where it joins the single line needs
to be big enough for you to place your ski within the 'V'
while waiting in the water for take-off. Also, once you start
to get under way the ski must not catch the narrow part of
the 'V' or this will, of course, tip you off.

Ready in the   Let us assume that you have the correct equipment. We
water   can now move on to the deep water start on one ski. Firstly
make sure your front foot is well and truly in the binding
either before or at the moment of dropping into the water.
Once you are in deep water allow the other leg, the one
that will eventually go into the rear bridge, to float free of
the ski. You will in fact use this as a rudder or counter
balance during the actual take-off. I will explain this in
more detail further on, but while it is not a rule I have
found that it is a great help to most novice skiers. When
you feel comfortable in the water, allow the rope to extend
slowly to its full length as the driver pulls ahead. Once the
rope is fully extended the skier will find that he has now
something rigid to hold onto and if he is slightly out of
position it will be easier to correct now. If you feel happy
then allow the ski to float up so that the tip is just showing
above the water inside the 'V' of the rope. It is possible
that to get the tip of the ski just out of the water you may
have to lean back in the water, but once the ski starts to
float into position then you should be back in the position
as shown in Fig. 19 with the leading leg well bent at the
knee.

Before moving away from the skier to the boat driver so
that they are both at the same stage in the take off, I had
better deal with the problem of the fellow who does not
have the right equipment and whose rope has only a small
'V'. So my friend you are unable to get the ski inside the
'V'. My advice is to go out and buy a new rope or if you are
able alter the one you have as it will save much time and

68

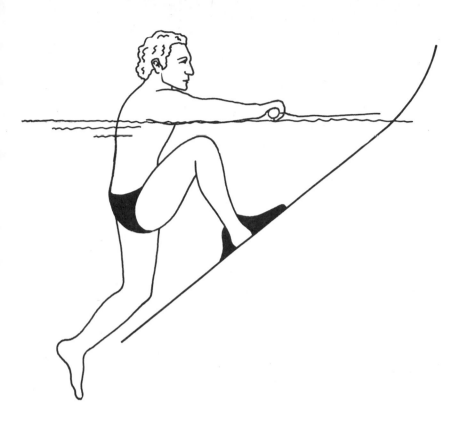

19   Correct position ready for one ski take-off from deep water

effort in the long run. However, it is possible to get up with
a small 'V', but as you have to keep the rope to one side of
the ski, this puts you off balance before you start. The best
advice here if you are going to persist in using this type of
rope is to lean the front of the ski gently against the rope.
This will help balance you but has the problem that at the
actual point where the boat starts to pull you through the
water the knot or shackle where the rope joins the handle
section is liable to catch on the ski. This is a point to watch,
but otherwise all you have to remember is that the rope
will be slightly to one side and obviously you will have to
adjust this as you start to rise from the water. As you can
see it is just an extra point to have to remember when you
least want anything further to think about.

The driver's role for a deep water take-off

Once you are sure the skier is in the water with his ski on and is ready to receive the ski rope, get your rope handler to throw the rope directly, but just over the head, of the skier. The art is to throw it far enough so it lands behind the skier and not on his head. This may seem a simple task, but if the rope lands too far out of reach it causes all sorts of complications for a skier on a mono ski in deep water. Let us take it for granted that your rope handler has the knack of throwing the rope within reach of the skier and the rope and skier have made contact.

Now slowly pull forward in a straight line until the slack is taken up and the skier is able to use the rope as a lever to correct his position. While it is the skier who will call for you to start your pull, you have a certain responsibility in making sure that you are ready to pull directly ahead as soon as he shouts. As with all types of boat driving for skiing the engine, if an outboard, must be straight or, if an inboard, the rudder must be stationed directly to go ahead and the way must be clear ahead for a good distance. It is worth remembering that this particular start is liable to take much longer and so you will travel much further before the skier is out of the water and planing than for almost any other type of start. If you have any doubt regarding clearance straight ahead hold the skier in position by slowly pulling ahead until the obstruction has moved away or, if it is static use this slow method of pulling slightly to alter your direction and give you ample clearance ahead.

Tidal waters

As with doubles skiing and the other deep water starts, tidal waters make life much more difficult. Always drive against the tidal flow for stability. Take into consideration that this deep water start is much more tiring for the skier, so when you are in tidal waters the quicker you are able to pull the skier out of the water the better. The important point, both in tidal and non-tidal waters, is to have the skier on a taut rope so any movement you have to make with the boat to compensate for conditions is automatically transmitted through the rope to the skier. Whatever happens, whether you have problems with the tide or another craft in the way, both the boat and the skier must be in a straight line at the point of opening up the throttle for take-off. If it is hopeless and you cannot achieve this tell the skier to let go of the rope and circle around and start again; it will be quicker and certainly much safer in the end.

When all is in line and the skier has called it is 'all systems go'. Open up the throttle with a steady, but quick action; do not jerk the boat forward, but give it much more power than for pulling a skier on two skis. You will certainly feel the extra pull from the skier. Be careful as this could pull you off course the first few times, but once you get the feel of the boat with this particular start you will find it easy to compensate for any sideways pull. Get your observer to watch the skier and give you a running commentary on his progress. Keep the throttle open wide as the skier pulls through the water and do not ease off until he is well and truly out of the water. Then the 'golden rule' comes into operation—when you ease back the throttle do it very gently and as smoothly as you can. It is worth thinking of the way in which you let out the clutch on a car to engage the gear. If you do it too fast the car will jerk and then stall. Exactly the same will happen to the skier if you alter the throttle position too quickly—the rope will jerk and as it takes up again it will stall the speed of the ski and pull the skier forward over the front of the ski. It takes as much practice for the driver to get a deep water one ski take-off correctly as it does for the skier, but always consider that the poor skier is getting a soaking each time either of you make a mistake.

Meanwhile at the skier's end of the rope, if all is well the boat driver has you on a taut rope. You are in charge, so give your signal and await reaction as they say. As the boat starts to pull slowly at first this is the time to make sure you are correctly balanced and all your odd parts, such as fingers and thumbs etc., are free of the rope. If the boat is powerful enough you will find the much gentler pull easy to control, but I must admit that in most cases the boat needs all the spare power it can muster. You may find that in this case, while the driver is giving it all he's got, you do not appear to be getting anywhere. This may only last a few seconds, but it can feel like hours when you have what appears to be a typhoon sized wave ploughing off the front

Under way with the deep water start

of your ski and for some reason at least fifty per cent of the water is driving straight into your face. The driver has been warned about this, so he may decide you are on the verge of drowning and abort the attempt. There must be a happy medium where you can stand this for so long, and if you feel the driver is slowing down too soon you must get together and perhaps try next time for a little further. It could, however, be the driver's fault as he did not give the boat enough throttle so perhaps you both need a little more practice. Still, try again and perhaps this time you will start to rise from the deep in all your new found glory. All is not won yet, however, because you will find that once out of the water you are still not planing fast enough to have full control over the ski.

I have moved on a little quickly in telling you what to expect after the initial pull, but if at the same time you take into consideration the following advice you will find it easier to correct your position should you lose your balance.

Holding the handle can be very important. There are two methods:

a. Hold the handle straight in front of you (see Fig. 20a).

b. Have the handle up against your body (see Fig. 20b).

Both obviously have advantages; the former method is usually the easiest to master if the boat has no problem with power, but it is liable to pull you over the front of the ski should there be any jerking from the boat. If the boat is slightly under-powered you may be forced to use method *b*, as this gives the boat that little extra pull at the point where the driver pushes the throttle open and before it takes the full weight of the skier. The method of holding the handle close to the body can make all the difference to the boat actually being able to pull a skier out of deep water. There is a knack when either using an under-powered boat or if you have very little space in which to take off, such as on a restricted lake—the idea is to bring the handle close into the body and turn both your ski and your body away from the boat at right angles. Allow the rope to run around the front of the tip of the ski which is just showing above the water and to pull against it. With one leg trailing outside the rear binding acting as a rudder, give your signal to the driver. As he opens up and the rope

20a   Grip mainly used in deep water and shallow water starts

20b   The best method of gripping handle for scooter and dock starts

snatches, turn quickly towards the direction of the boat. This has the action of pivoting you from the water and can speed your position from deep in the water to part planing in a split second instead of the usual drag through the water. This method should only be used when all else has failed or as I mentioned before, when you are so short of space that you need every inch of free water.

I have already mentioned how you can drag behind the leg which is normally in the rear binding to act as a rudder on take-off. This is a big help on all deep water take-offs, but you will find that if you are using a very powerful boat you can be pulled with both feet in the bindings. Many skiers always start from deep water with this leg trailing, as it not only acts as a rudder, but also as a counter balance should you start to sway before you are settled on the plane. I, along with many other skiers, do not bother to put my rear foot into the binding until I am well under way, even though I may rest it gently on the rear of the ski. I move it into the rear bridge when I know all is well. It may sound as though this is a long, drawn out procedure, but in fact it takes only a few seconds and I certainly find it a help.

Up and away   Once you have mastered the take-off and you are planing on one ski you will get a feeling very similar to that very first time you ever skied on two skis. It is very exciting to know that you can now take off from deep water and it is especially good to know you can now dispense with the 'drop-off ski'. Unfortunately, however, you are still in limbo between where you were after dropping off one ski in the earlier method of starting and the position from which you have risen from the deep on one ski. In the latter method you still have one leg dragging and with the drop-off method you are still unsteady with only one foot firmly in the front binding. This moment is critical as to lose your balance now means that you will almost certainly fall at an angle instead of sliding which is the usual way of falling when mono skiing, after you have perfected your take-off. To save these awkward falls you will have to practice correcting any wavering from a straight line. What usually happens is that the ski starts to pull to one side and you try and correct your balance by

74

leaning. This rights the ski and brings it and you back into a straight line behind the boat. However, most beginners overdo this lean to correct and find that the ski shoots off in the opposite direction. You can imagine that if this action is repeated only two or three times it can result in an uncontrollable wobble and throws the skier off. It may look rather funny to spectators, but it is not fun for the skier who either falls most uncomfortably or lands in a rather twisted position which can best be described as an ungainly posture. It is important to lean and pull on the rope to correct a sway, but do not lean too far or pull too hard; take it easy and if you feel you are losing control, let go of the rope and gently come to rest.

It is possible that you may pass through this stage of your take-off without problems several times and then all of a sudden you start to lose it. You may feel the rope is jerking once you are planing and this could be due to the driver easing off on the throttle too quickly, thus leaving you a little slack in the rope. It is best to have a diplomatic word with him about this when he comes around to pick you up for another try.

Once you have mastered the technique of actually pulling up into the planing position, and you are confident that you will stay upright, bring the trailing leg gently onto the ski and then into the binding all in you own good time. Do not transfer all the weight onto your rear foot until you are perfectly happy with your balance. The rear foot should by now be right into the rear binding, the firmer the better as later you will need this firmness to help you control when turning sharply once outside the wake. Mono skiing is much easier than it appears at first once you are able to transfer the weight to the rear foot. It makes the overall control of the ski much easier and you will feel for the first time after first learning to mono ski that it is you and not the ski that is in control. Although this transference of weight needs to be a smooth action it also should be done quickly. The less time spent passing through this stage the less chance you have of losing your balance and being thrown off, either due to the rope becoming slack or rough water catching you unawares.

When you are a beginner the description 'dry land   **Dry land starts**

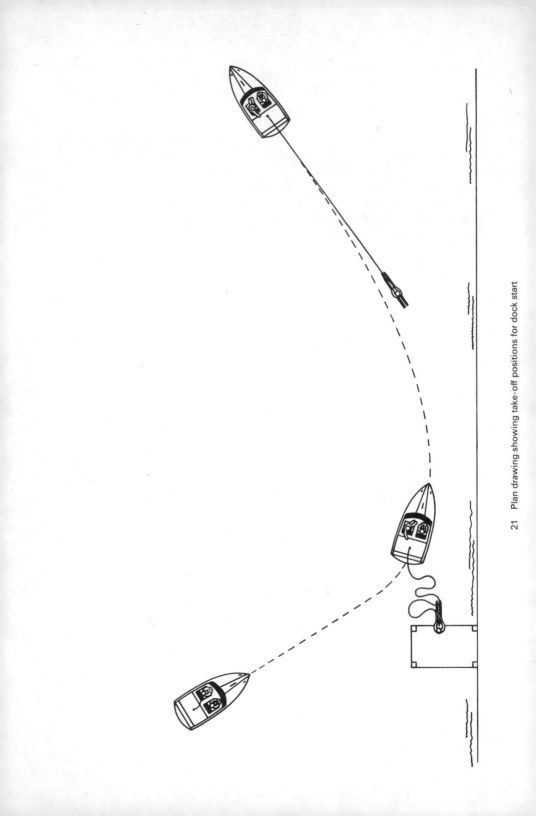

21 Plan drawing showing take-off positions for dock start

starts' will be far removed from what actually happens, especially on the first few attempts. You will quickly learn there are many more ways to dive into the water than those recognised by the various swimming and diving associations around the world. Still with practice it is undoubtedly the most rewarding way of launching yourself onto one ski and planing behind the boat without either too much effort and, when you are proficient, on most occasions without actually getting wet.

Dock, pier and raft starts

These types of starts are usual for all competitions as there is normally a take-off raft or dock on site. If the boat is really powerful, as a competition ski boat would be, then it is a fairly simple method of starting. Also of course, in the competition class of skiing, both the skier and the boat driver are very experienced and they will make the whole operation look so simple that one is inclined to feel it is the only practical method of starting. Do not be fooled, however, as there are many hidden snags so approach this method with caution and do not become over confident if you have already mastered deep water take-offs. Later on, though, you should find taking off from a dock or pier much easier than any other type of start. Taking all things into consideration, if the facilities are available, there is no doubt that it is the best method of starting on one ski. It can be done at sea or even on a lake by using a small rubber boat instead of a pre-fixed staging, but remember this will not be as stable as the latter and can have a nasty habit of drooping when you sit on the side to await the take-off.

As with the scooter start, later on, the timing has to be exact in order to save the skier from a ducking although a nose-dive may not be as painful as the meeting of nose and sand. However, the boat driver must be very careful to open up at the right moment or the skier will be slowly dragged into the water and what should have been a dry dock start will change rapidly into a very wet deep water start. Even at the best-run competitions this error receives a larger round of applause than anything that happens during the actual competition.

The driver

While the skier waits on the dock, (we will call it a dock from now on whether it be a dock, raft, pier or rubber boat) the driver and his rope handler circle in front of the dock. When they are called in as everyone is ready for the take-off the driver will pull away to one side and slowly run in a few feet away from the dock, but level with it, as in Fig. 21, making sure he is not too close to the skier. As the boat approaches the skier on the dock the rope handler must coil the rope so that he can throw the loose end with the handle on to the skier who will be only a few feet away. Once the rope has been thrown and caught by the skier then the boat will turn slowly away to take up a position directly ahead of the skier, but moving slowly forward. If the rope handler notices any problems with the skier on the dock then it is fairly simple for the skier to hold the boat in position by holding the rope taut while he sorts himself out as long as the driver puts the gear lever into neutral.

If all is well and the skier shouts, the driver will only have to open up the throttle and the skier will be pulled from the dock straight into a skiing position. As with most starts the problem for the driver is to make sure he goes at the moment the skier shouts or he will simply pull the skier from the dock. It only needs a few practice runs with a good rope handler to make this operation a fairly simple method of starting from the driver's point of view.

The skier

The skier has to practice a little harder before he can dry start from a dock each time without the many problems that can crop up whilst sitting perfectly dry on a dock waiting for the moment when the boat pulls you either on or into the water, according to the amount of experience you have had.

Once again the skier is in charge of the whole operation, but he will find there is so much more time to get settled that the whole manoeuvre from start to finish will seem much easier than any take-off on one ski he has learnt so far, especially since the original method of dropping one ski from two.

Just settle on the pier or dock with one ski resting on the surface of the water. Obviously you have to have a dock of the right height; it is no good trying to launch yourself from a pier with a 10 ft. (3 m) drop to the water! You can, however, take-off from a dock where your ski is just above the water. This is not too difficult. Stay on the dock with your ski just above the surface in a sitting position and as the boat takes up the slack in the rope just edge over the side of the dock so that you are only just balancing on the edge. With luck you can still make a good dry take-off, but the timing has to be exact as it is rather difficult to retrieve a good position if for some reason there is a moment's delay in the boat getting under way at full power. It is also fraught with danger as not only are you liable to slip into the water but wooden docks and piers are well known for their total disregard as to where they lodge their splinters should the boat snatch you a moment before you are ready. Rule One—try to find the correct height in a launching pad (see Fig. 22).

Let us presume that all is at the right height, your ski is resting on the surface and the boat has passed just in front of you. The rope has gently landed in your lap and the boat is now pulling slowly directly in front of you as in Fig. 21. Make sure you are on the edge of the dock and that you are holding the handle ready for the pull as shown in Fig. 20b. Once the rope is almost taut, shout to the driver and, providing he has followed the instructions correctly, he will open up the throttle and the boat should pull you away easily from the dock. I mentioned earlier that one of the advantages of this type of start was that you had more time to get into a correct or comfortable position. It also has the advantage that while most skiers prefer the rope handler to let the rope out slowly to the skier it is just as practical for him to pass over all of the rope and you can coil it with you on the dock. The problems with this are of course that you can become tangled up with the rope, but at the same time should the boat be slightly under-powered you may need a few coils of the rope just before take-off as with the scooter start. A worthwhile point to note is that with this start you can start with both feet in the ski. Some find it easier to start like this while many top skiers still prefer to keep one foot trailing until they know all is well with the take-off. Also be careful that the deep fin of the mono ski is not lodged on a cross member under the dock on which you are sitting. If this happens you will depart without the ski and almost certainly get your first taste of barefoot skiing. Finally if you should make a mistake with the timing then you can still allow the boat to

22a   One ski dock start. Ready to go

22b   Moment of take-off

22c   Pulling through the water

22d   All systems go

pull you off the dock. Just hang on and drop into an ordinary deep water start. You may find that the first few times you try this take-off you will partly do this anyway. It is better than allowing too much slack in the rope and being pulled over the front of the ski.

The scooter start

It is only fair to warn you that many skiers give up when trying to learn what is known as the 'scooter start'. Still perseverance is the keyword and if you and the driver make up your minds not to give up after several abortive, but spectacular, spills you will soon master this type of take-off and all will be well satisfied with the effort.

This method is mainly used from the shoreline or at least where there is a gradual incline away from dry land to the water. Not only do you need to stand in around one foot (.5 m) of water, but it is also very important for the ski boat to be in deep enough water while only about 60 ft. (20 m) away from the shore. As the boat driver and his rope handler play such an important part in this operation I will describe their role in detail first before moving on to that of the skier.

Boat handling for dry land starts

Before doing any skiing in an area it is, of course, advisable to drive slowly over the area, as already mentioned. When driving for a skier attempting scooter starts it is essential for both to study the proposed skiing area and, if possible, to know something about the bottom of the sea or lake. The boat has to come in close to the shore for take-off and for dropping off the skier after a run. The skier cannot come out too deep or he will have trouble getting clean away on take-off, but the boat has to come in close enough to give a straight pull. More than ever it is important to remember that the stern of the boat will dig in deep at the moment of take-off. Certainly if I am skiing in an unfamiliar area I always try a couple of mock starts before going ahead to make sure that there is no underwater obstruction around the boat's position on take-off. It is surprising how often around the coast the sand slopes gently away for some distance, then builds again further out. Sandbanks which are out of sight can cause many problems, both to the boat's propeller and the skier's nose should he dive over the front of the ski at the moment of launching. This digging in of the stern is very pronounced, especially, if you happen to use an outboard-powered boat. You will also find that the inexperienced skier will try to hold on even if he has not got it altogether right at the start and this holds the stern down deep much longer than is normal with an experienced skier.

Once you are sure of the skiing area then the driver needs to take particular note of what the skier is trying to achieve. The vital moment of take-off will be as much under the control of the driver as the skier. Too much throttle, or not enough, will certainly ruin any attempt. Timing and cooperation between the skier and driver is the only possible way of achieving this type of take-off.

In Fig. 8 you will see how to approach the skier and pass the rope from the boat to him. In most cases the skier will be standing in shallow water without the ski on, so the actual throwing of the rope need not be as accurate as with the deep water take-off. Once the skier has retrieved the rope, however, there is much for him to do before the boat has moved out into position for take-off. As always tidal waters make the whole operation much more difficult, but it is worth remembering that, on receiving the rope, the skier has to put on his ski, coil the rope and then obtain a balanced position on one leg before being ready to call for take-off. During this time the driver has to move slowly away ahead of the skier, arriving in the correct position at the right time. If he is too early the skier will find the rope has become taut before he is ready and it will almost certainly pull him off balance or, as usually happens, he will have to let go of the rope. Then the whole operation has to start again right from the beginning. To move out too slowly can also cause problems, especially in tidal waters where the drift can only be countered by using the power of the boat. As no doubt you will have found some time ago a power boat is very difficult to control without using the throttle. It is much harder to control when you have a skier standing on solid ground and holding onto a ski rope attached to your boat. Let us not labour the point any further, but remember that to get this start correct we must make sure the boat arrives at the point where full power needs to be applied when the skier is ready to shout for take-off. If the driver has followed

23a Preparing for a scooter start

these instructions and moved into position as shown in Fig. 8 then it is time to move on to the skier's side of the operation and bring them both together further on.

'Scooter starts' – the skier

It is usually easier to carry the ski into the water and put it on when still in shallow water. Once you have reached a point where the water is just under knee deep, and the boat can come within 20 ft. (6 m) of you without grounding, then you should be ready for the scooter or 'hop' start as it is sometimes called. Wait for the boat to circle in front of you and when in range the rope handler or observer will throw the rope to you. One reason for not having the ski on at this point is that the thrower may not be all that accurate and you may have to move quickly a short distance to retrieve the rope.

Once you have the rope you need to move fast, slip on your ski and stand on the bottom in order to keep your balance. The boat will now start to straighten up in front

23b Adjusting the ski and binding for scooter start

23c Correct position ready for the take-off

of you and will be pulling slowly forward. During this period you need to coil the spare rope loosely (see Fig. 24); you should have about 30 or 40 ft. (10 m) lying on the surface of the water. If you are quick enough you will be in position well before the boat has moved into the take-off position and in that case, you are in complete command of the operation from now on (see Fig. 23).

Let us go through the procedure step by step:

1. Allow the rope to become taut and hold the boat in a straight line in front of you.
2. Let the rope slide through your hands as the boat pulls slowly ahead, still keeping both feet on the bottom.

24a   Handling the rope ready for a scooter start

3. Allow this operation to continue until you are left with three loose coils of rope in one hand. The remainder of the rope should be straight and taut between you and the boat.
4. Bring the foot with the ski onto the surface with the ski actually resting on the surface so that you are balancing on one foot (see Fig. 23). The tautness of the rope in front of you should help you to keep your balance.
5. In one movement, as soon as you feel you are ready and well balanced, throw away the loose coils of the rope, move your spare hand over to the handle as in Fig. 24b and then shout for take-off to your boat driver.

24b Throwing away the slack prior to take-off

The timing of all the above movements is very important and if at any time you feel you are losing control of the situation, either by losing your balance, the fin of the ski getting stuck in the sand (this often happens to inexperienced skiers) or, most important of all, if the boat is out of position, then throw the rope away. It is easy enough for the driver to go around again and start the operation from the beginning, but it is very difficult to regain control whilst hopping about on one foot up to your knees in water.

If all is well the boat will start to pull away very fast as it has a few feet of loose rope and nothing to hold it back. You will have gathered by now that at any second you are going to receive a hefty pull forwards and the high speed of the boat will be dramatically reduced. When this happens the skier usually comes off second-best and nose-dives over the front of the ski. This normally gives the spectators on the beach a good laugh and the skier a sand-papered nose. The knack is to throw only enough rope away to allow you to shout at the correct moment so that the boat takes up that spare slack and gets you on to the plane without too much of a jerk. The power of the boat and experience will resolve this problem, but you must be prepared for some ungraceful departures from the ski until you have succeeded. If you have a really powerful boat you may need to throw only half a coil away and be pulled off with an already taut rope, but this is rare when using the usual family ski boat. Again it is possible that the boat in this type of take-off will need some assistance from the skier. The skier may have to give a couple of hops at the moment of take-off even after allowing for three coils of free rope before the boat takes up the slack. With practice all will come together and when you do get that jerk as the rope takes up it will become less and less painful as time goes on.

After your shout there will be a few seconds before the tension is taken up on the rope; these seconds are vital so make the most of them. Here are the rules:
1. Grip the rope with both hands and pull into the body as in Fig. 20b.
2. Push the ski hard against the surface, but keep the tip up and remember to make sure the fin has not dug into the sand.

25 Fully equipped
with buoyancy aid
and helmet ready for
slalom course

3. Lean back with your elbows in to take the pull of the boat as in Fig. 23c.

You will find by following these simple rules that the speed of the various actions will ensure that they all come together automatically, but it is still something of a shock when you take up the tension and suddenly find you are launched onto the surface of the water. You may even find you are doing everything right, but after the initial shock pull you appear to move only a short distance forward before falling. Firstly check to make sure that you are deep enough and that the fin is not hitting the sand, then secondly, that the boat is not losing too much power at the moment it takes the extra drag from the skier. (If I may include the driver here, it is worth taking into consideration that both a heavy, experienced skier and a light beginner will cause the boat more problems than you may notice from the controls. Also, you must open up the throttle of the boat as soon as you hear the skier shout or the drag will come too soon and the skier will not have a chance to retrieve the situation.)

Up and away

Once you are away do not be in too great a hurry to put your trailing foot into the rear binding. Use it as a rudder as in deep water starts. It is a great help both in retaining your balance and in correcting it should the ski start to pull away to one side. Once you are sure you are away and correctly balanced slide your foot into the rear binding with an easy movement as with most one ski take-offs. The great advantage of scooter starts is that with experience you can execute a dry start from a shoreline and, with the exception of a little spray whilst skiing keep reasonably dry throughout your ski. Much will depend not only on making a successful take-off from the shallow water, but also on the timing of the release of the rope at the end of your ski run.

**Mono skiing –
once up . . .**

You may ask what is the difference between mono skiing and slalom skiing. To be honest, there really is no difference but for the sake of simplicity when teaching it is easier to describe the method as mono skiing. Slalom skiing does not really occur until you are further advanced and start to ski around slalom buoys, as I will describe briefly later on. To keep the subject simple we will move on to what happens on one ski once you are up after either a one ski start or after dropping one ski after being on two.

Let us presume that you have now mastered the take-off and you are skiing in a straight or almost straight line behind the boat, a bit wobbly perhaps but you are hanging on there. Remember you have smoothly slid your rear foot into the rear bridge and you feel fairly comfortable. As when learning pairs skiing give it time and just stay inside the wake for a few runs. By all means try leaning over, but not too drastically to start with. If you fall from a mono ski you either nose dive over the front or you over-slide. Also, just to keep you in a planing position the boat must be travelling faster than when skiing on a pair so it is probable that if you fall you will make contact with the water with greater speed. To put it in plain language you will not only make a much bigger splash, but you may hurt yourself.

Now that you are feeling fine and your confidence is building up, you may try pulling and leaning to either the left or right to pull to the outside of the wake. In fact you will almost certainly find that actually to cross the wake on

26 Mono skier really leaning into turn

one ski is easier to control than on two. This is because if you are in the correct mono skiing position (see Fig. 26) you will be standing back on the ski. You have a firmer grip on the rope and as long as the boat's speed is constant and the rope stays taut then you should have much more control than you had on two skis, when the slightest change of speed through rough water or boat handling is reflected through the rope and you find yourself with slack rope. This control is demonstrated by the incredible angles at which top slalom skiers find themselves when skiing around the buoys of a slalom course (see Fig. 27).

To start the run across the wake, try leaning away from the boat, say, to the left; this will bring the ski around at an angle to the boat and will propel you away to the left of the boat and then across the wake. This is the easiest part as it is more difficult to turn the ski back to re-cross the wake. Once you are outside keep to the well-tried formula of taking it easy. Gently pull on the rope, turning the ski towards the direction of the boat and bring your body up into a more upright position. Still lean back on the ski, but not to the side. At this point you will be travelling along following the course of the boat, but outside the wake (see

27 Rounding buoy on slalom course

28 Slalom skiing outside the wake

Fig. 28). To start the move back either into the wake or to run right over both peaks of the wake and out to the other side, then lean gently in towards the wake and the ski will come around and once again propel you towards the wake. After a number of practice runs you will start to change from leaning away from the boat and towards it almost at once on the outside of the wake, as you would on a slalom course. However, be careful always to make sure that you have a taut rope as the momentum while you pull to the outside of the wake can build up easily without you realising it and when you arrive at the point of no return right outside the boat, you may find you are overtaking it. This is known in water skiing terms as 'having a handful of slack'. Not only will the rope go slack as you overtake the boat, but you will start to slow down and begin to sink while the rope is still slack. It does not take much imagination to realise what will happen when the boat catches up, the slack is taken up in the rope and you are still holding on half under water. There is an old Air Force saying 'when in doubt, jump out'; this is never more apt than when you find yourself in such a position in water skiing. When you get really competent you will almost certainly do just that for the sheer fun, but it is not recommended for beginners.

Once you have gradually improved your style on one ski and gained the confidence to lean over hard on the corners you will find much more enjoyment than you ever did when skiing on two skis. Practice combined with experience gives you greater satisfaction, but learn more than one way of taking off. If perhaps you learn first the deep water method, then master not only the take-off, but the mono skiing afterwards and then try the other starts. It is worth noting that at some time in the future you may be on vacation where the only take-off point is from shallow water, where you will need the scooter start or from a dock where you need a pier or dock start. It will ruin your enjoyment if you find that you have to revert to two skis just because you are not sure of the other take-off methods. Very few ski schools at vacation areas like to use the drop off method because of the chance of losing one of their skis.

With practice you may also feel confident enough to join a water ski club and try your hand on a slalom course. This is water skiing in a different world and the only real way to improve in slalom skiing is to be coached on the spot. This can either be achieved through a club or various water ski federations throughout the world which offer short period 'teach in's' where if you have the aptitude you can advance further up to competition level. I do not think it is possible to put in writing the ways to improve when you have reached the point where you are happy at general mono skiing and have mastered the various take-off techniques. So as far as getting up and skiing on one ski is concerned this is as far as this book can go. However, as I never like to keep a reader in suspense or mono skiing around the lake for ever, I will just finish by giving a few hints both to the skier and the driver on how to get off after a mono ski run.

Coming in to land

It is of course, basically the same method for both the driver and the skier as it is for skiing on two skis. There are, however, a few hidden snags and it will save a fair amount of coming to grief after a successful run if you are not only aware of the problems, but also take note of them.

The driver

When the skier has indicated he has had enough then

proceed to the drop off area using exactly the same easy sweep as for any skier whether a beginner, improver or expert as in Fig. 17. You will have already found much more drag towing a monoskier than when towing a skier on two skis. The stern of your boat, unless it is of exceptional power, will be pulled much deeper into the water than normal, both on the initial thrust on take-off and while skiing. This will be very noticeable on cornering and one should always take corners very easily both for the sake of the skier and to be sure that you do not flip your boat over. The point at which a skier suddenly finds he has a lot of slack rope is the most dangerous time in skiing. If he holds on, the forthcoming snatch will certainly be a big strain on the boat, especially if it is angled on a turn. The second moment of danger is when the skier lets go of the rope, either on purpose or because of a fall and the boat is suddenly let loose after being under immense tension. At this point the boat is usually out of control so the golden rule must be to take it very gently on all turns.

As you come in for your final run be careful if the skier is on the outside of the wake on the side on which he is due to land. If you are too close in, as he is using a mono ski with a deep fin, he will almost certainly be thrown off if he catches an underwater obstruction or touches the bottom. Once the skier has let go the boat will be released like a cork out of a bottle of champagne so make sure that there is plenty of free water in front of you.

As for the driver you will also find that the procedure for coming in to land is exactly the same as on two skis (see Fig. 18). The main differences, however, are:

The skier, landing

a. You have a deep fin under the ski. Not only is this liable to catch any underwater obstruction, but when it grounds on the bottom it usually stops you dead. On two skis you have a fair chance of stopping in a standing position, but if the fin digs into sand you will almost certainly part company with the ski. Remember you are in shallow water so the result can be rather painful.

b. When you let go of the rope at the end of a run you will sink almost at once. On two skis you carry on planing for a fair distance and if you let go in too deep water you can often have time to change direction and actually stop in shallow water. On a mono ski you will stop so

95

quickly that if you have misjudged the distance to the shore you may have a long swim. Still, it is better to under estimate and swim than to come in too close and find the ski stopping before you do.

c. It is a good thing to try and land where you started as you will remember the boat driver has already checked out the area so you have a good idea of what is under the water.

Once again it is not only practice and experience which are needed, but cooperation between skier and driver. You will find that most drivers are skiers and vice versa on two skis, but with mono skiing this does not happen so often so it is up to the skier to make sure that his driver is not only well briefed, but is aware of all the pitfalls.

Part Four
ADVANCED WATER SKIING

Once you have reached the standard in mono skiing where you can start from most of the recognised take-off positions and you are able to ski well once you are up, you will be at a cross-roads in your water skiing enjoyment. If you are young and the facilities are available you may join a water ski club. If you do you will almost certainly improve on your mono-skiing by trying your skill on a slalom course. From there you can take up jumping and figure skiing but to be an expert at any of these three advanced techniques you need to be dedicated to the sport. Throughout the world, unfortunately, facilities for practice, allowing a young skier to advance to even national level, are scarce. To be one of the élite who ski at international level not only requires perfect facilities, dedication and a first class coach, but it also helps tremendously if the weather can be relied upon. Still great trees from little acorns grow, so do not let me put you off as these facilities although few, are available in most countries. With the sponsorship of large business concerns and often government help a youngster can be trained to reach the top even in the so-called 'cold water' countries.

Most water skiers when they arrive at this point in their water skiing tend to carry on and enjoy the freedom of the sport and steer away from the competition side. Families often ski together until father bows out, then the son takes over and in turn teaches his children to ski. This is the basic ingredient for deriving full enjoyment out of water skiing as it is with most other sports. The teaching or passing on of knowledge gained through experience over a number of years can be just as rewarding as winning championships. I know even today I still feel a great deal

29 World Champion Mike Hazelwood performing one ski turn over wake

of satisfaction in teaching a 'first-timer' at water skiing.

As I mentioned earlier, I feel that once a skier has advanced to mastering mono skiing, to progress further they move from being taught to being coached. This is a personal relationship between sportsmen and while one can often put into book form the basic techniques it can often be more of a hindrance than a help to the coach who may appear later on the scene. He may have to get rid of bad habits in the way you approach a particular manoeuvre so I will mention only briefly the other more skilled techniques of water skiing.

Jumping

I will cover jumping first as it very rarely concerns the water skier who is not a club skier. The ramps used in jumping are difficult to maintain and the conditions under which they have to be used limit them to club use. Also, safety and the power of the boat needed to keep on line correctly for jumping dictates that a person would be ill-advised to try jumping without strict supervision.

It is a great spectator sport and whether you wish to try

it or leave it to the more daring, it is still well worth a visit to see the top water ski jumpers in the world as they soar over 150 ft. (45 m) from the ramp. The falls are naturally spectacular and especially so amongst the beginners, although the real hum-dingers occur when the world champions are trying for that extra inch at international meetings. Just to wet your appetite I have included a picture of a skier jumping in Fig. 30.

The greatest single thing about figure or trick skiing is that you can do it behind most family ski boats and all you need is the correct skis as shown in Fig. 31. The danger is proportionate to water skiing on one or two skis and the enjoyment gained by doing the most simple of tricks is worth all the effort. Not only will you need to practice for hours on end, but in some of the tricks you will have to endure the laughter of your friends at the antics you will get up to in trying to achieve even an upright stance. Still, the enjoyment of water skiing is in the trying and as I will

Figure or trick skiing

30　M. Cazzaniga of Italy in full flight, jumping at World Waterski Championships, England 1975

31 James Carne in backward position having performed 180° turn on two skis

only describe the easiest tricks we can look upon this operation as doing it 'just for the laughs'.

Before moving on I feel I should define the difference between trick and figure skiing. Though there is no official definition the simplest way to express it would be to say that the competition skier is figure skiing whilst other skiers are really just trick skiing. It is possible of course that some of the simple tricks are just a manoeuvre on the way to figure skiing. What I am about to describe is really trick skiing and we will leave the figure skiing techniques to the experienced coaches.

Backward take-offs

When I first started water skiing most trick skiers started by learning the 'Backward take-off from deep water'. This in itself is not difficult, but it does need endurance. It also helps you get the feel of skiing backwards which is a peculiar feeling for the first few times (Fig. 31).

The sequence for the driver is the same as any deep

water or shoreline start with the boat circling in front of the skier and taking up position as in Fig. 8. The skier takes up position in the same way as for the ordinary deep or shoreline start, but he needs to be wearing trick or figure skis as shown in Fig. 31.

Once the boat has run out the full length of the rope (you may need a shorter rope than usual for trick skiing if the wake of the boat peaks in the wrong place) then sit back with the skis in position as usual as in Fig. 7a. When the boat has taken up the slack in the rope and it is idling forward turn in the water, passing the rope behind your back. At this point the driver must be very careful not to pull the skier off balance, but just keep the rope taut. The next movement takes plenty of practice and a great deal of courage. Lower the handle below the back of your knees, keeping a very firm grip on it. As you do this you will be forced to bend your knees and in turn this will make you duck your head underwater. I know it is difficult not only to achieve that position, but also hold it (and read this book at the same time), but this is exactly what you must do. Allow the skis to float up into a take-off position, still keeping the handle tucked in behind your knees and your head underwater. O.K. Hold it, while I have a word with the driver.

Once you, or your observer, has seen the skier do his or her duck-dive wait until the skis appear in the take-off position. They must be level and this is not easy for the skier to get right the first few times, so you may have to hold it there while he comes up for air and has another try. On seeing the skis in the correct position start to pull forward very steadily for the first few yards and if the skier is still in position then accelerate away, but a little slower than for a normal deep water forward take-off.

By this time the skier may have decided that life was not worth living anyway and his past will have shot before his eyes. Actually, it is surprising how long a skier can stay in that position as he is working to place the skis correctly. Once you feel the boat start to pull you then you will know your skis are in the correct position and it is 'all systems go'. As the speed starts to increase you will rise from the water, admittedly rather ungainly but nevertheless you will surely rise. If you will pardon the expression you will be in a 'bottoms up' position with your face just above the water. This is rather nerve-racking as you see the water shooting past your nose and you are going backwards into the unknown at what appears to be a great rate of knots. Still hold on.

After a few seconds in this position you will gradually be able to straighten up, but do this gently. The boat has to give only a slight judder at this point and it will undoubtedly pull you over backwards. Once you are comfortable and skiing along backwards with your hands still gripping the handle behind your knees, then slowly move the handle up until it is in the small of your back as in Fig. 31. Let me pass on a tip here; it is better to lean further away from the boat than to be too upright. You will find this a help should the rope jerk at all during this delicate operation.

On finding yourself skiing backwards, give vent to your feelings and yell 'Eureka' or something similar; this will not only make you feel better, but it will draw attention to your feat.

Rather strangely more difficult than actually skiing backwards is deciding how to finish off your run. The first few times you can just let go of the rope and sink, then practice a few more starts. After a while though, you can start trying to turn around from back to front and adopting the normal forward skiing position.

180° turns

It was thought in the early days of water skiing that it was easier to turn from back to front than from front to back. Some still think so, but I must admit that clubs these days do not bother about backward take-offs and they teach from front to back. This, I feel, comes under the coaching side of water skiing, but it can add to your enjoyment if you can ski both backwards and forwards and turn from one to the other.

Side-slides

Most skiers before attempting to make a 180° turn try side-sliding on the skis first. This is fairly simple, but needs concentration and a will to succeed. You have to make sure the skis are parallel to the boat; if they are at an angle you will move away from inside the wake and un-doubtedly lose the sideways motion. In Fig. 32 the skier is

actually moving into a side-slide before dropping into a 180° turn. He of course is on one ski, but the positioning is the same. You will note his arms are well bent. This is very important on side slides and turns as the rope handle has to be close to the body on turning. If it is not, the handle will be out of reach when you have made the turn, especially from front to back.

Other figures
Once you have achieved the art of turning a 180° turn in both directions and perfected the side-slide there are plenty more for you to try, but at this point you are really moving into the realms of figure skiing. From 180° on two skis you will progress to 360° turns and then through all these tricks again on one ski. Then, on two and one ski you will try the same figures on, in and over the wake of the boat. A one ski turn over the wake is shown in Fig. 32. As you progress the figures become harder and, if you are lucky enough to have the time and the determination to practice, you may advance to going through all the figures again, but with toe-holds as shown in Fig. 33. You certainly do not learn these difficult feats from books, but the ultimate aim at this stage is to put as many of these figures together in one run in each direction in front of judges who will mark with points each trick or figure and when you start scoring around the 3,000 point mark you can say you have arrived on the international water skiing scene. Mind you that is not enough to win, but you will be coming along quite well.

Fun behind the boat for the family skier
As a final few words in this book I should like to remind you that there are plenty of other watery pursuits in which you can become involved with a water ski boat. These can be great fun and often can be enjoyed by members of the family or friends who for some reason are unable to water ski.

Aquaplanes
Young children love to ride on what have become known as Aquaplanes. These are made of either plywood or a plastic material and the rope is attached to the actual board. They are towed directly by the boat and with an extension rope coming from the upper surface of the board the rider can then stand up and be towed along. These are ideal for very young children as not only will aquaplanes

float, but they can be towed at very slow speeds.

Skim-discs

The skim-disc is not so popular now as it was a few years ago; this may be because of the cost. Skim-discs are round, about 4½ ft. (1.35 m) in diameter, and the skier stands on it and holds the ski rope as in water skiing. The technique in getting up on the disc in the first place calls for plenty of practice as it is quite a scramble from a prone position through to kneeling and then standing. Once there, however, you can turn the disc and ski backwards and from there advance to a comedy routine for your local regatta. I know friends who have taken their dogs for rides and even ridden on the top of step-ladders perched on an extra large disc.

Surfboards

Since the demise of the disc the surfboard has been used more for having fun behind a ski boat. One way is to use the full length ski rope and lay prone on the surfboard. Once you are underway at skiing speed you can stand on the board and use it like a giant mono ski. This is called

Freeboarding

'Freeboarding' and you may often see surfers doing it behind a friend's boat when the surf is flat.

If you feel like a real laugh with a surfboard, get a couple of friends to do scooter starts on two separate mono skis while you do the same on the surfboard. Once, or if, you are all up and two are mono skiing and you are freeboarding then allow one of the skiers to come alongside you and step onto the surfboard, dropping his ski, but retaining the rope. Then the other skier can do the same thing. With a powerful boat you can fit five or six riders on an old fashioned 'big gun' surfboard. Mind you, it only needs one to start laughing and the shakes which are then transmitted through the board will throw it out of control, landing you all in the water.

Wake surfing

This not only needs considerable skill, but the boat must throw up a really good shaped wake to make this sport worthwhile. It is very important to get the persons in the boat sitting in the right position to make a decent wake about 10 ft. (3 m) behind the boat when travelling at just below planing speed. This is the point where the boat wants to get up and go, but it must be held at that speed in that position to create a large curling wake behind the boat.

The person on the surfboard (it is again best to have a large 'big gun' board about 8 to 9 ft. (2.5 m) in length) holds the ski rope, but this time it is shortened to just enough to allow the rider when standing to be just behind the wake. Once again lie in a prone position and when you are moving at the correct speed and the wake is correct, move into a kneeling position and then into a standing one with one foot in front of the other. The stance is similar to that of a surfrider when riding on waves. Pull on the rope until the board goes over the top of the wake and starts to run down the face. Once there hold it in that position.

By trimming the board, moving forward to speed it up or back to slow it up you will find that you can hold a position on the wake and you do not need the rope. Once you are in this position throw the rope to someone in the boat and you can carry on almost indefinitely. If the boat needs to be turned, it must turn very steadily towards the side on which the surfer is riding. This is possible with practice on the part of both the driver and the rider. It is also possible to speed the board up towards the boat and cross from one wake to the other, but only with a limited type of craft where the wake is high, but flat on the top. This is usually with a large inboard boat or even a cruiser where the wake is naturally large and some way behind the boat. It may appear to be dangerous as you are near to the boat, but if you do fall it is almost certain that the forward motion of the boat and the stability of your surfboard will drop you in the water well behind the boat. One word of warning to the driver—if the rider falls, the wash behind the boat will catch up with you so be prepared to open up and drive away from the wash when this happens. Your boat will be very low at the stern, especially if it is an outboard as the passengers will be in the rear seats to create the large wake needed for wake-surfing.

Kites and para-kiting

I do not intend to go into the subject of kiting and para-kiting which is flying a parachute behind a speedboat, as there has been considerable controversy over the high accident rate. All I will say is that it needs a really powerful boat and both your kite and equipment needs to be in first class order. Using an up-draught parachute behind a boat is not as dangerous, but it is not very popular and I know of only a few places around the world where it can be watched regularly.

Making the most of your ski boat

As you will see there is plenty more to water skiing than just being pulled around the bay on a pair of water skis. You can use a whole range of accessories such as aquaplanes, discs, surfboards etc. as well as the different types of water skis. Most need plenty of practice, but in all except the competition stakes skiing is more fun than dedication.

I suppose I should close this book by just expressing a desire that you enjoy your water skiing whether it be in a warm or cold climate. It matters not if you ski on the sea, on a river or on a lake as long as you remember that the major consideration is safety and that you spare a thought for all the other water users who may not appreciate water skiing. There has always been a certain amount of bad feeling between water skiers and yachtsmen as there is between fishermen and canoeists, but we have to live together so perhaps a thought for the problems involved in the other fellow's sport is the order of the day. Local authorities are the real culprits in many cases as they often ban certain sports rather than simply controlling them. Nothing is worse than having to tell a boat owner that he is unable to tow a water skier in an area for almost certainly he will break the law and do his water skiing where it is most dangerous and upset other water users. With control he may be curtailed, but at least he knows that the area is reserved for that particular sport.

Let us hope that the text of this book has helped in some small way to add to the enjoyment water skiing can bring to family and friends. You never know perhaps your son or daughter or even you, may be tempted to try water skiing and end up a champion. Not all want to take the sport seriously, but as long as you get enjoyment from being in the outdoors and we achieve some measure of satisfaction from your performance then, with safety in mind, you will find water skiing well worthwhile.

List of Federations and Associations

American Water Ski Association
State Route 550 and Carl.
Floyd Road,
Winter Haven, Florida 33880, U.S.A.

Australian Water Ski Association
Box 111 Post Office,
Pascoe Vale South,
Victoria 3044, Australia

British Water Ski Federation
70 Brompton Road,
London, S.W.3, England

Canadian Water Ski Association
333 River Road,
Place Vanier,
Vanier City,
Ontario, Canada

Fédération Francaise de Ski Nautique
Bld. Pereire 9
Paris 17 ème, France

Fédération Italienne de Ski Nautique
Via Piranesi 44B
Milan, Italy

New Zealand Water Ski Association
518 Queen Street,
Auckland, New Zealand

Venezuela Water Ski Federation
Final Avenida Libertador,
Esquina Bello Campo,
Caracas, Venezuela

Index